IMAGES
of America

HANSON

This book is dedicated to Raymond H. Towne (February 20, 1918–July 25, 2002), Hanson's first official town historian. He served from February 23, 1999, until July 25, 2002. His wealth of knowledge of Hanson's past and his willingness to share his stories with both young and old are keenly missed.

The book is further dedicated to Elsie G. Calder (April 15, 1895–June 13, 1991), a teacher in the public schools for 44 years. She was born in the home at 819 Main Street, where she maintained her residence all of her life. After retirement, she tutored from her home. She was a charter member, secretary, and treasurer of the Hanson Historical Society. She is well remembered for her writings on the history of Hanson, including her book *Looking Back*. She is shown here at the age of seven.

IMAGES
of America

HANSON

Donna McCulloch Brown

ARCADIA
PUBLISHING

Published by Arcadia Publishing,
Charleston, South Carolina

Library of Congress Catalog Card Number: 2003106111

For all general information, contact Arcadia Publishing:
Telephone 843-853-2070
Fax 843-853-0044
E-mail sales@arcadiapublishing.com
For customer service and orders:
Toll-free 1-888-313-2665

Visit us on the Internet at www.arcadiapublishing.com.

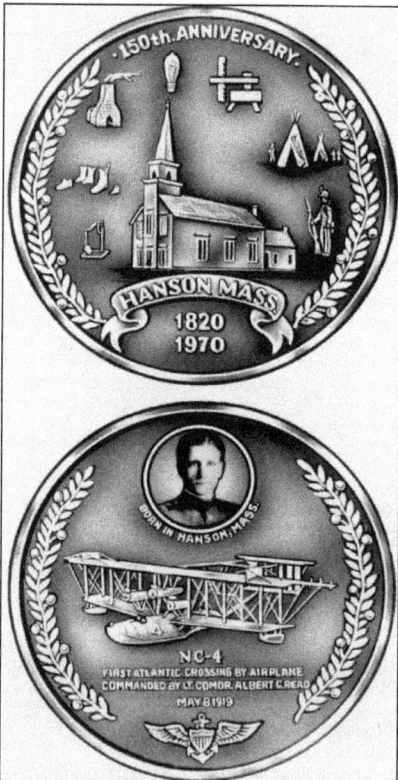

Flanked by cranberry vines representing the town's largest industry, the commemorative coin from Hanson's 150th anniversary depicts the Congregational church with early industries around it. These include a lumber mill, an iron furnace, a machine for manufacturing nails, the electric light bulb industry, and the shoemaking trade. The wigwams represent Hanson's earliest settlers, and the military figure symbolizes the formation of the Hanson Light Infantry in 1820. The reverse side is a tribute to Lt. Comdr. Albert Cushing Read, who made the first successful transatlantic flight.

CONTENTS

ACKNOWLEDGMENTS

Hanson is very fortunate to have an active and hardworking historical society that makes the effort to treasure and share its extensive collections of photographs. At weekly meetings over the last four months, Hanson Historical Society curator Rodney Brunsell helped choose photographs that would be just right, shared his extensive postcard collection, and spent endless hours editing copy; graphic designer Norman Forgit assisted with making the final choices based on the quality of the pictures; and Allan Clemons shared his vast knowledge of the residents and antique homes in town. My sincere thanks go to each of them.

Bruce Young, writer of a weekly column in the *Hanson Express*, supplied historical information. Wes Blauss, a Hanson middle school teacher who is active at Camp Kiwanee, worked on the introduction and provided camp history. Hanson teacher Jennifer Taylor, my daughter, edited and proofread the manuscript. David Hickey, another Arcadia author, helped with the layout. Whitman-Hanson High School senior Katie Jordan, through the work-release program, worked several months on the projects, and junior Bethany Forrest also contributed. My employer, New England Art, allowed me a flexible work schedule, and my coworkers offered interest and support. I am grateful for their contributions.

The following people shared their photographs or memories: Ellen Stillman, Silvia Salas, Jude Braley, Harold Ibbitson, Harold Towne, William Briard, Richard and Betty Landis, Joanne and Walter Estes, Esther and Kenneth MacKenzie, Edna and Henry Howland, Roland and Marie Morse, Louise and Bill Scott, Paul J. and Patricia A. Dias, Barbara Brunsell, Judy Forgit, Joanne Blauss, Natalie Powell, and John Campbell. Their generosity is appreciated.

Thanks also go to the Hanson Congregational Church, Linda Archibald; Leighton's Funeral Home, Marjorie Leighton; Red Acres Farm, Gret Lozeau; Olde Hitching Post, Arthur and Joan Leanos; Heidi's Hollow, Linda and Tony Quigley; Lite Control, Anne Marie Yankin; Hanson Airport, John Sweeney, John Duffy, and Chip Diggins; Rainbow Camp for Girls, Nancy Noyes; Clayton's Texaco station, Clayton Prario; Ferry's Sunoco station, Jack Ferry; the Hanson Police Department, Chief Edward Savage III; the Hanson Fire Department, Chief Allen Hoyt; Hanson firefighter Jerry Thompson; and the Ocean Spray Cranberries Inc. archives, Chris Hormell.

Always, special thanks and love go to my husband, Dannie "Skip" Brown, who works two jobs so that I can undertake volunteer projects that are dear to my heart.

INTRODUCTION

The first people settled on the northwest shore of Monponsett Pond 4,000 years ago. They dressed in animal skins and hunted with spears, never imagining the advent of the bow and arrow. Long after them came the Algonkins, crossing the *Tunk* (a walking wall, bridge, or path) through the great cedar swamps connecting Mattakeesett (now Pembroke) and Satuckett (East Bridgewater). They surveyed their hunting grounds and could not foresee the coming of the white man and the end of a century's-old way of life. The English separatists who settled here never suspected they would one day separate from their mother country and forge a new nation. Riding the inaugural run of the Old Colony Railroad in 1844, Massachusetts statesmen Daniel Webster and John Quincy Adams looked out on the rural farming communities through which they passed, marveling at this new technology that sped them down the rails from Boston to Plymouth in a single afternoon, hardly envisioning the Industrial Revolution and the sprawl of suburbia that would eventually overtake the land. Gradually, change came to the land and the people who lived on it, and that change resulted in the community of Hanson.

By the 1600s, the original ownership of the land was in dispute between Massasoit, sachem of the Wampanoags, and Chickatawbut, sachem of the Massachusetts tribe. Pilgrim descendant Maj. Josiah Winslow and 34 others purchased a large tract of land from Chickatawbut's son, Josiah Wampatuck, on July 9, 1662. For some 75 years prior to incorporation, the future town of Hanson was called the West Parish of Pembroke. The first white settlers cleared and cultivated the land for hay, corn, and potatoes. A mill was constructed on the dam site at the foot of a pond that now bears Wampatuck's name. Horse-drawn vehicles and ox carts hauled cords of wood for shingles and rail fences from the cedar swamps. Iron ore was mined from the local lakes and waterways. The industrious farmer turned every available acre to some use, and the wife at her hearth prepared meals of porridge and Indian pudding, succotash, brown bread, boiled pork or beef with potatoes and pumpkins, and on Saturday a real treat, salted fish, was served.

By the 18th century, a motley collection of shingle weavers, coopers, carpenters, tanners, weavers, shoemakers, and a tavern owner, Ebenezer Bonney, were hard at work in the area. A sawmill, a tack mill, a smithy, and an iron foundry produced the stock necessary for the growth of a town. The town grew quiet and disquiet as well. The ordination of the Reverend Gad Hitchcock to the Congregational church of the West Parish presaged the Revolutionary era. Invited to deliver the election sermon of 1774 at the Old South Church in Boston, the local minister took as his text Proverbs 29:2, "When the wicked beareth rule, the people mourn." An enraged Gen. Thomas Gage sat in the audience, fingering his sword, but Samuel Adams and other Boston patriots presented Hitchcock with a new suit of clothes in appreciation. The minister, his son, and other local boys served in the Revolutionary War and are buried in Fern Hill Cemetery.

Dissatisfaction over parish lines resulted in the incorporation of a new town 50 years later. By an act of legislature passed February 22, 1820, the West Parish of Pembroke became the town of Hanson, a name selected in honor of Alexander Conte Hanson, Baltimore editor of the *Federal Republican* newspaper, whose antiwar stance in 1812 provoked a mob of infuriated Republicans to attack the press. Cannons were dragged in, men were killed, and when Hanson and several others were jailed for their own safety, the mob stormed the building and threw Hanson down a flight of stone steps, leaving him for dead. He survived, crippled, and continued the fight for freedom of the press, and in 1816, with tempers cooled and public sentiment changed, he was elected to the United States Senate. His death three years later at the age of 33 inspired the residents of this new town to name their community after him. Hanson represented rights that the people in New England believed to the depths of their souls—freedom of the press and speech.

In each war that followed, the homespun men and women from Hanson participated to protect those and other freedoms for themselves and for their country. Until World War II, Hanson was a simple farming community. Shoemaking remained a cottage industry, and the railroad facilitated the growth of cranberry cooperatives and production of porcelain lights, dyes, and other goods. However, change came with the spread of highways and the progress of transportation. Suburbia spread south from Boston, and today, the town is a bedroom community for hundreds of commuters traveling by train and car to jobs in the city. Like earlier inhabitants, residents of today cannot clearly envision what the future holds for Hanson.

In the following pages, moments from the past are captured in photographs. With the history of the area spanning over four millennia, these photographs encompass only 100 years or so, a brief period of life in the town now called Hanson. Thankfully, in that short time professional photographers and amateur camera buffs caught a glimpse of the history that reminds us who we were and who we are today. This is a fragment of our story, but these images may help us imagine our past. As author Thornton Wilder says in *Our Town*, "So—people a thousand years from now—this is the way we were in the provinces north of New York [in the] twentieth century. This is the way we were: in our growing up and in our marrying and in our living and in our dying."

This a view from the air of the center of the town of Hanson. When Chip Diggins of Middleboro attended a "fly-in" at the Hanson Airport, he let me share a ride with him in his experimental airplane so that I could reflect on the beauty of Hanson. My thoughts were of the people who first saw this beauty, the founding fathers of this area. Surely they were as awestruck then as I was in 2003. Hanson is indeed a town to treasure.

One

PUBLIC PLACES

In 1872, Abington builder Charles Bonney constructed the first and only town hall building near the bank of the Wampatuck Pond at 542 Liberty Street. This stately Victorian structure was built for the sum of $8,506.50. Annual fairs, old home days, and the Hanson Brass Band concerts were held on the town grounds. Community activities and musical concerts are still held on the grounds. Horace Atwood, a local builder and for many years the building inspector, completed an annex on the right side in 1942. The town's growth led to a large architecturally compatible addition on the left side, which was dedicated in 1999.

The Civil War Monument was once located at the entrance of Fern Hill Cemetery. The monument was dedicated on October 20, 1906 to the soldiers who enlisted in Hanson and the Hanson men who enlisted in other localities. It was moved to the west lawn of the town hall in 1925.

The Fern Hill Cemetery is located on High Street. Entrance to the cemetery is gained through the granite archway, which was erected in the early 1900s through the efforts of the Hanson Improvement Society. Directly through the archway can be seen the Civil War Monument, which was moved to the west lawn of the town hall in 1925. Standing at the archway in this 1905 photograph is Flora Bourne Washburn.

Thomas Hall was a popular building erected on West Washington Street in 1884 at a cost of about $3,500, paid for chiefly by the generosity of Elijah C. Thomas and his sister, Rachel C. Cushing. The upper floor was finely equipped for drama and musical entertainments. Plays were performed and enjoyed here off and on for almost a century. The lower floor offered a banquet hall and a large room for a library. After faithfully serving as a community building for over a century, the building met a tragic end by arson on August 1, 1991.

On the first floor of Thomas Hall was the library, which was formally incorporated in 1884 as the Hanson Library Association. By 1902, more than 1,500 volumes of choice books graced its shelves. During the early decades, the librarian was Mary J. Drew.

A SALE AND FAIR

---WILL BE HELD AT---

THOMAS HALL, HANSON,

Thursday and Friday Evenings,
November 16 and 17, 1899,

Under the Auspices of

THE HANSON IMPROVEMENT SOCIETY.

All Persons Interested in the Arch, to be placed at the Entrance of Fern Hill Cemetery, will please Come and Patronize the TABLES, where will be the usual attractions, consisting of Fancy Articles, Aprons, Farm Produce, Peanut Grab, Guessing Cake, Candy--- ALL of WHICH will be EXCHANGED for LUCRE.

Various Articles Will Be Donated To Persons Showing The Best Judgement In Guessing.

DON'T FORGET TO DIG IN THE KLONDYKE!

THURSDAY EVENING,
Our Dark Friends Will Be With Us, And They Will More Than Amuse You. Come One! Come All!

FRIDAY EVENING,
Vocal And Instrumental Music, Readings, Etc., Followed By A Laughable Farce, Entitled, "BLUNDERING BILL."

ADMISSION   -   -   -   -   10 CTS.

SEVERANCE PRINTING CO., So. Hanover, Mass.

THE LAST RALLY.

WILL BE HELD

AT

THOMAS HALL HANSON

Monday Ev'g. Nov. 3 1890.

THE FOLLOWING SPEAKERS ARE ENGAGED.

Mr. O. L. Bonney, for the Democratic party,

Mr. H. H. Packer, for the Prohibition party.

Mr. S. Mc Allister, for the Republican party.

Music by a Quartette.

COME DEMOCRAT.   COME PROHIBITION,
COME REPUBLICAN.   COME EVERYBODY.

Speaking commences at 7 45

Shown are two Thomas Hall handbills listing upcoming activities. The one on the left announces a Sale and Fair to be held the evenings of November 16 and 17, 1899. Notice the 10¢ charge for admission. The hall was raising money for the archway to be placed at Fern Hill Cemetery. The handbill on the right is for the Last Rally, a political speaking engagement complete with musical entertainment.

HANSON LIB. ASSO. ROOM

This sign was used on the Hanson library room door on the first floor of Thomas Hall until the library relocated c. 1900 to the home of its librarian, Mary Drew.

12

These handbills show two more examples of events held at Thomas Hall. The one on the left is for a Thanksgiving Musicale run by the Hanson Socialist Club, with an admission charge of 15¢. The one on the right is for an Entertainment and Sale, with an admission fee of 10¢.

It is hard to believe that one could attend this Concert and Ball for the sum of 20¢. From today's perspective, almost a century later, eerything in 1910 seems very inexpensive.

The Plymouth County Hospital was built by order of the county commissioners under the direction of Boston architect J. William Beals. Construction began in 1917 and was completed in 1919. Dedication exercises were held on May 31, 1919, and the first patients were admitted on June 16. The hospital treated patients with tuberculosis. It was located on Bonney Hill on the line of electrics that ran between Brockton and Plymouth, within a 15-minute walk to the South Hanson Railroad Station.

Christmas postcards sent greetings from the Plymouth County Hospital in 1930. Decorating for the holiday and posing for this card would have been enjoyable Christmas projects for some of the young patients.

The Plymouth County Hospital thought at one time that fresh air in all seasons was one of the cures for pulmonary tuberculosis. In this photograph are children outside in the snow without shirts playing London Bridge Is Falling Down. The theory was later disproved.

The nursing staff is shown on the steps of the Plymouth County Hospital. Notice they are all dressed in their white starched uniforms and caps. Muriel Ripley MacLellan is fifth from the left, and Barbara Ripley Briard is third from the right. The rest of the nurses are unidentified.

Post Office, Monponsett, Mass.

The new Monponsett post office opened on July 6, 1912. Arthur L. Willett served as its first postmaster. Located across from Monponsett Railroad Station, the office served both permanent and summer residents of the popular and scenic lakes region, which encompasses the southern part of Hanson and the northern region of Halifax. The post office is still in operation, but is now housed in a newer Cape-style building at 935 Monponsett Street.

The post office stood on the north side of Main Street at what was known as Post Office Square. Nan Harley was the postmaster of the South Hanson post office c. 1907. Her assistant and only employee was her husband, Fred Harley, who was also the only rural mail carrier. For many years, he faithfully carried the mail by wagon, sleigh, and, sometimes, foot when the snow was too deep for the horse to plow through.

16

Two

Fire and Police

Shown is the Hanson Fire Department Hose Company No. 2 fire wagon from the South Station, located on Main Street. From left to right are Edward Keene, Norman MacKenzie, Will Thayer, Angus MacLellan, Irving Bryant, Charles Burrell, Fred Brown, Ben Livermore, James Lowery, Sumner Josselyn, John Ibbitson (driver), Merritt Bates, and Ibbitson's horses Fred and Dick. This photograph was taken in 1912 in front of United Cape Cod Cranberry Company, later known as Ocean Spray Cranberry Company, also on Main Street.

Fred and Dick pull the Hanson Fire Department Hose Company No. 2 fire wagon. The wagon was transporting six call firemen in the early 1900s.

This No. 2 fire wagon was from the South Station, on Main Street. From left to right are firemen Charles Burrell, Arthur Brown, Fred Brown, and Sumner Josselyn; James Lowery, in the driver's seat; Norman MacKenzie; and horses Fred and Dick.

This is an early motor vehicle of the Hanson Fire Department. From left to right are John Ibbitson, Roderick McClellan, Arthur G. Brown, Ben Livermore, Irvin Bryant, and Fred Brown.

This 1910 photograph shows the first fire engine from Hose Company No. 3 in Burrage. It was one of the first fire trucks in the state used to fight forest fires. From left to right are Joseph Dowler, John Jewel, Charles Raby, John Thompson, and James Apply.

This concert and ball was likely a fund-raising event for the new Hose Company No. 1 fire station, built in 1909 at Harding's Corner, just down Washington Street from Thomas Hall. Storekeeper Walter Calder and his daughter, teacher Elsie Calder, preserved this wonderful old broadside and many other fine Hanson paper items over the last century.

A Hanson father and son are shown in 1939. On the left is patrolman Kenneth MacKenzie, who became the second police chief, and on the right is his father, Norman MacKenzie, the deputy fire chief.

20

The South Station, located on Main Street, is shown here. The fire engine is a Seagraves from the late 1940s.

The fire department was very proud of its lineup of fire trucks. This picture was taken in 1958. Shown are two Seagraves, a 1941 Mack, and three Dodge Power Wagons from 1952 to 1957.

This photograph was taken in front of South Station to celebrate the purchase of the second-hand ambulance in 1955. Notice the enlargement of the station doors. From left to right are the following: (front row) Jack Casoli, George Ford Jr., Frances Hannon, Lloyd Prario, Raymond Reid, Everett Ford, Robert Brown, and Loring Hammond; (back row) Norman McDonald, Edmund Benson, Harold Ibbitson, Phillip Robichaud (fire chief), Kenneth MacKenzie (police chief), Bob Anderson, Robert Andrews (selectman), unidentified, Norman MacKenzie, unidentified, Irving Foster, Wilson Brooks, unidentified, Garland Brooks, and Elwood Prario. The 1949 Ford Woody wagon (left) belonged to Garland Brooks.

The fire department's call firefighters are pictured with three fire engines in front of the South Station, on Main Street. South Station was built by James Bourne in 1915. The engine on the left was from the South Station, the engine in the middle from Burrage Station, and the engine on the right from North Station.

A large illegal alcohol distilling plant, or moonshine still, was located off Hudson Street near Poor Meadow River *c.* 1923. The continuous hauling of heavy loads of supplies on Elm Street aroused the suspicion of Hanson's chief of police John H. Ibbitson (left foreground). After investigating, Ibbitson contacted the Bureau of Internal Revenue and a successful raid was held. Shown with Ibbitson, from left to right are officer Fred Brown, Whitman's chief of police Leroy Phinney, and officers Cyril Ibbitson, Franklin Phinney, and Edwin Churchill.

John H. Ibbitson (left) stands with five of his fellow officers in this 1920s photograph. Ibbitson was chief of police in Hanson from 1922 to 1946.

23

The Hanson Police Department gathers for a group picture. From left to right are the following: (front row) E.E. Churchill, J.A. McClellan, J.H. Ibbitson (chief), K. MacKenzie, and E. Foster; (back row) P. Robichaud, J. Taylor, C. Ibbitson, and R. McNamara.

A testimonial dinner for retiring Hanson chief of police John Ibbitson was held in the dining room of the National Cranberry Association, in South Hanson, in March 1947. From left to right are the following: (front row) Leroy Phinney (retired Whitman police chief), Eben Towns (a lawyer), Marcus Urann (president of the United Cape Cod Cranberry Company), Ibbitson, John Geogan (a Whitman lawyer), and Norman G. MacDonald (a Hanson businessman); (back row) Warren Mitchell (a probation officer), Arthur Sullivan (a court clerk), Robert Clark (assistant district attorney), Mike Stewart (Scituate chief of police), J.J. Avery (Quincy chief of police), Jimmy Moore (Bridgewater chief of police), and Albert Brouilard (a state police lieutenant).

Bob Brown is shown here in his police uniform. Brown was also a highway surveyor for 20 years and a firefighter. His father was also on the police force, as shown below.

Fred Brown is seen serving as a motorcycle policeman for the Hanson Police Department. He is half of another father-son team of civil servants, as his son Bob Brown was also a policeman.

Kenneth MacKenzie was born on November 28, 1914, the son of Norman and Elizabeth MacKenzie, who lived on High Street. He served as a Hanson motorcycle patrolman until he entered the U.S. Army, where he served in the military police. MacKenzie was appointed the chief of police for Hanson upon his return from the service in 1946. He lives on Main Street with his wife, Esther, who was raised in Duxbury. MacKenzie retired in 1971. He is shown here directing traffic for the 200th anniversary of the First Congregational Church in 1948.

Three

EDUCATION AND FAITH

This is one of the first kindergarten classes from the early 1900s. From left to right are the following: (front row) Edwin Thayer, Carrie Howland, Marie Beals, Annie Richards, Grace Josselyn, Clara Langill (teacher), Dorris Calder, and Carl Swanson; (back row) Sara Calder, John MacDonald, and Hayward Stevens. The school was at 142 High Street, on the corner of High Street and Pierce Avenue. The house in the background was the home of Clinton Calder.

The No. 4 primary school was located on Beals Hill near 1308 Main Street at the time of this photograph. Mary Howland (Kilbreth) was the teacher from 1898 to 1900. From left to right are the following students: (front row) Hollis Ibbitson, two unidentified students, Laura Stuart, Abbie Monroe, William Benoit, Seward Brown, Fred Brown, and Robert Calder; (middle row) Mary Stuart, unidentified, Minnie Crocker, Mamie Crocker, Sadie Ford, Martha Everson, Nina Chamberlain, Marie Davis, Edgar Monroe, and Howard Sampson; (back row) Myron Stuart, Oliver Brissett, Felix Brissett, Harold Brown, Harry Hill, David Brissett, Della Benoit, Lizzie Strang, and Doris King.

This photograph of a No. 4 primary school class, with teacher Grace Delano (background), was taken on October 7, 1903. From left to right are the following students: (front row) Mary McDonald, Marion Sampson, Mildred Monroe, Flora Wright, Hollis Ibbitson, Weston Crocker, Mary Valley, Arthur Valley, Chester Richards, Edwin Ibbitson, Hattie Kinsington, Toofler White, and George Ford; (middle row) Seward Brown, Giles McDonald, Ralph Harley, George Faulkner, Florina Valley, Abby Monroe, Florence Hobill, Mildred Ibbitson, Emily DiMestico, Fred Brown, Joseph Tillson, Loring Besse, Russell Richards, and George DiMestico; (back row) Arthur Richards, Jessie McLain, Josie Hill, Elsie Calder, Edgar Tillson, Edith Kinsington, Adlor White, and Nelson Burrell.

The No. 4 primary schoolhouse, built in 1845, was located at 43 Elm Street. In 1867, it was moved to Beal's Hill on Main Street. In 1939, it was moved to the L.Z. Thomas School on Main Street and used as a fourth-grade classroom. In 1962, it was moved to the other side of the L.Z. Thomas School by Francis Kenneally. It was reopened as the Hanson Historical Society on October 3, 1963. A three-seater that remained behind the Thomas Hall for over 70 years was donated and moved to the grounds in 1965. A shoemaker shop, built in the 19th century, was donated by Mae and Frank Grieves and dedicated to Antone Slaney on September 12, 1981. The No. 4 schoolhouse is the oldest remaining schoolhouse that continues its educational role. It has been selected for nomination to the National Register of Historic Places.

The No. 5 primary school was located at 190 West Washington Street in North Hanson. The school was later remodeled as a residence at the same location.

The South Grammar School was built in 1881 at the site on which the Grange Hall now stands. The school was moved in 1907 to property on Reed Street that was donated by the Hanson Manufacturing Company and was reopened as Primary School No. 7. From left to right in this 1903 photograph are the following: (front row) two unidentified students, Bernice Cogan, two unidentified students, Sadie Ford, Marie Davis, Nina Chamberlain, Robert Calder, Wesley Besse, two unidentified students, and Stuart Chamberlain; (middle row) unidentified, Maud Brewster, Lillian Ellis, Doris King, Martha Everson, unidentified, Lillie Hammond, Bert Hammond, Joseph King, Edgar Monroe, and four unidentified students; (back row) Royce Josselyn, Henry Straffin, Leon Everson, Burton Clark, Anna Witt (teacher), unidentified, Oliver Brissett, two unidentified students, and Harold Brown.

This class picture is from the South Grammar School. From left to right are the following: (front row) Harry Bearce, Tony Pennini, unidentified, Ralph Harley, Robert Bearce, Parker Wilson, Fred Brown, unidentified, Jennifer Harvey, Bertha Thomas, Loring Besse, and George Willis; (middle row) Roland Hammond, Arthur Richards, George DiMestico, Hollis Ibbitson, Theodore Hammond, Bert Hammond, George Faulkner, Mildred Wilson, Frank Pennini, Weston Crocker, unidentified, Seward Brown, unidentified, Robert Calder, Elsie Calder, unidentified, and Abbie Monroe; (back row) Marinda Crocker, Ruth Collins, Nelson Burrell, unidentified, Emma Sampson, Marion Sampson, unidentified, and Grace Delano (teacher).

The 1947 graduation of the eighth grade was held at the L.Z. Thomas School on Main Street. From left to right are the following: (front row) Helen Willet, Jean Fernandez, Laura Benoit, Margaret Turner, Eleanor Bates, Joanne Brooks, Roberta Lundberg, Lorraine Tassinari, Claire MacDonald, Anne Close, Dorothy Coffey, Joline Snow, and Ellen Cushing; (middle row) Alan Sayce, Les Metcalf, Walter Cunnigham, John Clarke Jr., William Ingalls Jr., Ralph Dill, Alfred Pina, Russell Mayer, Richard Ibbitson, and James Brine; (back row) Gerald Clancy, Donald Conway, Robert Gaudette, George Gilbert, Richard Freden, and Paul Harrington. In the background on the steps are John Weedon, Zillah Bryant (principal), and Mrs. Cote (an eighth-grade teacher).

Private kindergarten classes were held at the High Street home of teacher Leone Lemon (right). From left to right are students in the 1963 class: (front row) Joey Stearns, John Lunnin, Laurie McLaughlin, Jim Ferry, Lori Estes, and Kim Corey; (middle row) Ken Holmes, Bob Paine, unidentified, Chip Gassett, Jim Borghesani, Scott Braley, and John McNally; (back row) Heidi Reed, Julie McLaughlin, Nancy Wyman, Sharon Ibbitson, Jill Beaulieu, and Libby Richter.

This church congregation was formally organized on August 31, 1748, as the First Church of the West Parish, but the second church of Pembroke. When the West Parish became incorporated as the town of Hanson in 1820, the old meetinghouse became the First Congregational Church of Hanson. This current church building, at 639 High Street, was built at a cost of $3,113.26 and dedicated on December 14, 1836. The deeded rights to the pews were sold to parishioners for a total of $3,597.97.

The Hanson Congregational Church is shown in this photograph from the late 1880s. The first pastor was the Reverend Gad Hitchcock, who served for 55 years. To the left of the church is the carriage shed, where the men often gathered after services. The parish hall was completed in 1958. In 1998, the church held its 250th anniversary with a year of celebration.

The Hanson Congregational Church, at 639 High Street, is shown in this early 1900s photograph. It sits on Bonney Hill, where the elevation is at its highest in Hanson. The trolley tracks were installed in 1900.

Fr. Eugene A. Maguire purchased a tract of land at 25 Maquan Street near the junction of Maquan and Indian Head Streets. The purchase was made from Hanover Fireworks Company in July 1938. A year later, the church was dedicated to St. Joseph to serve the people of Hanson and Pembroke Lakes. On June 18, 1956, it was rededicated to St. Joseph the Worker. In 1981, the church held its 25th anniversary celebration.

The First Baptist Church added the tower, steeple, and bell *c.* 1850 under the leadership of Br. Asa Bronson. The chapel and vestry were added in 1875. A pipe organ was installed in 1890. The baptistery was added under the pulpit in 1903. The original pews were replaced in 1911. The original steeple was destroyed by a thunderstorm in 1951, and it was replaced that fall. The fellowship hall and Sunday school were added at the basement level in the early 1960s.

The First Baptist Church, located at 214 Main Street, was constructed in 1820, just as Hanson separated from Pembroke. The structure originally resembled a typical New England meetinghouse, without a tower and steeple. Elder Torrey was the first pastor and remained until 1825. The Baptist Church was the first to approve a temperance movement. It also took a stand against slavery and slaveholders as early as 1844.

Four

AROUND TOWN

This southward view on Liberty Street shows Hanson's town hall in the distance. Trolley wires are stretched over the tracks for the Plymouth and Brockton Street Railway that ran through Hanson from 1900 to 1925. The wood-shingled building on the right was a trolley stop called Dame's Waiting Room. Civil War veteran and storekeeper Albert Dame, of High Street, was also a successful postcard publisher of local views. For use as a waiting room, the Plymouth and Brockton Street Railway furnished Dame with free electricity for the building. As the trolley approached, the lights would dim. This building and property was later acquired by William Walkey for his various enterprises.

This eastward view shows Harding's Corner on Washington Street and the venerable general store (right foreground) run by Henry B. Harding. Soper's Hall, later the general store of Andrew Bowker, is next, followed by the only survivor, the fire station of Hose Company No. 1, built in 1909, now inactive. Note on the left the large cast-iron drinking fountain for man and beast.

This Harding's Corner photograph looks northward toward Spring Street from the intersections of East and West Washington Streets. People in their period outfits were gathered for yet another photographic opportunity.

This view, looking northward on Liberty Street, shows the Elijah Cushing House. By the 1920s, the house had been sold out of the Cushing family and served briefly as an antiques shop. During the 1930s and 1940s, a popular tearoom was featured here. In the snow on the left are the tracks of the Plymouth and Brockton Street Railway. The garage on the right was once operated as Keene & Estes, also as Fuller & Keene and, in this picture, as the Hanson Garage.

The intersection of Spring and Whitman Streets was known as Cox's Corner. In this 1914 view are two Cox homes. The one on the left, built in 1872, was renovated in the 1930s by the Boytano family. Other families that enjoyed this home include the Taylors and the Brunsells. The antique Cape on the right has had several owners, including the Cox, Thrasher, Turner, and Moen families. Note the trolley tracks of the Plymouth and Brockton Street Railway, which operated on this route from 1900 to 1925.

William and Eva Stillman purchased this home at 482 Elm Street in 1919. Both born in Lithuania, the couple met and married in the United States. William wanted to live in the country and finally found his dream in this home in Hanson. It was a fully operational dairy farm. The property included over 150 acres of land, a pond, and later, cranberry bogs. The Stillmans' daughter Ellen continues to run the Stillman estate—and its cranberry bogs—to this day.

This home of William Brewster was built in 1813 and burned in 1890. In 1897, Frank Keene built a new house at 396 Elm Street for Calvin Howland.

The Nelson Thomas home was located at 306 Pleasant Street. It stood in back of the store, which was built in 1907 by James Balboni. From left to right are Ruth Anne Thomas, Nelson Thomas and his wife, Elizabeth (who was blind), and Lizzie Thomas Paine.

The house at 65 Pleasant Street was built in 1877 to replace the home of Alfred Pardy, which was destroyed by fire. Flora Bourne Washburn is standing on the porch of her home.

Built in 1837–1838 by Thatcher Thomas, this was a typical old New England farmhouse. The house was located at 22 Main Street. It was first the home of Walter Damon and then of Heman Thomas, who changed the building in 1907 by building up over it. The ell was moved to Union Street for a residence, and the windmill was moved to Fred Snow's land. Another owner was Dr. Norman Breil.

The Damon house, located at 230 Main Street, replaced another Damon house that dated back before 1830. Elijah Damon constructed this house in the late 1850s. By the beginning of the 20th century, Hubert Gorham, a superintendent of a cranberry bog, owned this home and continued to live here until after 1930. The barn was severely damaged by the 1938 hurricane.

The home at 580 Main Street was built *c.* 1850 for Charles Howland. Other residents include the Kingman, Thompson, Hobill, Brewster, and Newey families.

The Deacon Daniel Crooker house, at 617 Main Street, was built in 1769. It was built as a two-room center-chimney Cape, with a barn, on 20 acres. The ell was moved to the property and attached *c.* 1800. The present barn was built *c.* 1850. This picture was given to the home's current owners by Brian Routledge (right, at about three years of age), whose parents, Margaret and Richard Routledge (left) owned the house from 1920 to 1928. This photograph was taken *c.* 1923.

The property at 847 Main Street was built in the winter of 1875–1876 by Gibson P. Beal, a carpenter. He added a barn 10 years later. The property was completely fenced in. Beals shared his home with his wife, Maria Beal. The Monroe cemetery is in the back of this property. The last person buried there was Cyphus Howard.

The home at 848 Main Street was built in 1852 by Benjamin Josselyn for Elihu Thomas. Notice the fiddle fence, which extended all the way past the property, and the electric car rails. The Thomas family lived here for many years. Later residents included Jessie and Walter Nealy, a chemist at Ocean Spray Cranberry Company.

The house at 1178 Main Street was built in 1902 by Frank Keene for his son Harry Keene. It was purchased in 1950 by Richard and Elizabeth Landis, who found the builder's name and the date written on the wall under the wallpaper.

Austin B. Howland built this home on Main Street for merchant Edwin T. Clark in 1894. At the time of this photograph, in 1912, the house was decorated for the 200th anniversary of Pembroke. It was then the home of Violet and Harold Clark. Harold Clark owned Clark's store for more than 50 years. He is shown in his driveway with his order cart and horse.

The Phillips-Keene house, at 1036 Main Street, was constructed in 1790 by Lot Phillips. By 1903, the property belonged to John Foster, who operated the nearby John Foster Company. It became the home of Agnes and Marcus Urann in the 1930s. Marcus Urann established the Ocean Spray Cranberry Company, which was located almost across the street. The home had a large greenhouse and beautiful gardens, including rose arbors. It was a sizable landscaped lot with a stone retaining wall surrounding the property's perimeter.

Marcus Urann, president of Ocean Spray Cranberry Company, owned one of the first automobiles in Hanson. It was an open car with bucket seats. He is shown driving his 1912 White roadster. With two leather button-tufted seats, the White was a heavier and more stylish and expensive automobile than those usually seen in rural America at that time.

This was called the Urann Pond when Marcus Urann owned the property on Main Street. Urann was president of the Ocean Spray Cranberry Company. In the background is Phillips Street. From left to right, enjoying their homemade boat, are Jimmy Shay, Eddie Clark (whose father owned Clark's Store), and Jackie Shay. The pond was a popular gathering place for ice-skating in the winter. Urann usually had lights set up so that people could skate at night.

The George Morton Crocker homestead is located at 1321 Main Street, at the corner of Elm Street. It was built by George Crocker and his father, Luther Crocker, in 1870. This picture was taken in 1890. George Crocker was a painter and paperhanger.

Walter Keene, builder and patternmaker, built his home and barn at 1209 Main Street in 1872. His windmill filled a large tank with water, and the family was one of the first to have running water in the kitchen sink. This picture was taken in 1890.

This is the residence of Walter A. Keene as it looked in 1885. W. Hallie Keene is standing by the fence. The Keene home was located at 1209 Main Street. The shed was later moved to 417 High Street.

Zero High Street was built in 1821 by Ebenezer Keene. It replaced a former house that was built for Alexander Soper as a tavern. The house remained in the Keene family into the early 20th century. One Keene family resident, W. Herbert Keene, was a photographer and took many early pictures of South Hanson. The house was in the news in 1874 when key evidence was found in a secret closet regarding the Sturtevant murder in Halifax.

The home at 321 High Street had many owners. Clayton White owned it and then sold it to John Scates, the town clerk and treasurer. The house burned after being struck by lightning in October 1923. Urban Boulanger built a new home on this land in 1924. Josie Estes, Hanson's music teacher, also lived here.

In 1722, Daniel Haywood built this historic Colonial home at 909 High Street, at the corner of Liberty Street. The Reverend Gad Hitchcock (1719–1803), a Harvard Class of 1743 member who was honored with a Harvard Doctor of Divinity degree in 1787, became the first pastor of the newly formed Congregational church and relocated to Hanson in 1749. His son, also Gad Hitchcock, became a physician, served as a surgeon in the Revolutionary War, and lived in the house until his death. The current occupants of the property are the East Bridgewater Savings Bank and the Hanson Insurance Agency.

Josiah Cushing built this home at 784 Indian Head Street in 1763, and it remained in the Cushing family for over 70 years. In 1837, the town of Hanson acquired the house and used it as the almshouse for the rest of that century. In 1902, the house was acquired by the Gordon Rest, a vacation home for working women run by the Massachusetts branch of the International Order of the King's Daughters and Sons. The almshouse was renamed the Sunny Side Cottage, or the E. Trask Hill Cottage, and used as an annex to the main building.

The home at 324 Winter Street was built in 1790 by Thomas Macomber. This picture was taken in 1940. The barn is still standing, but the home burned in 1981. A reproduction saltbox home was built by Dave Lefort on the same site in 1982.

This home was originally built in the center of Pembroke in the early 1800s. It was moved in 1860 to its present location, at 671 Indian Head Street, by Pamelee Howland. This picture was taken in 1940. Allan Clemons enlarged and remodeled the home between the years 1962 and 1980.

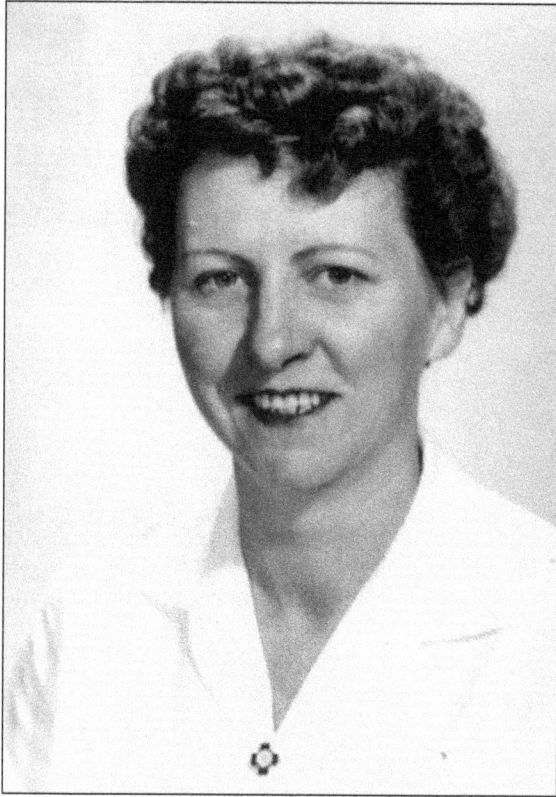

Jessie Morse was born on October 2, 1915. She lived at 22 Indian Head Street with her husband, Clifford Morse. She was the school nurse at the Indian Head School from 1949 until her retirement in 1983. After her death on August 26, 1983, the Indian Head School named the health department in her memory.

The home at 22 Indian Head Street was built in 1920. It sits on a beautiful piece of property beside the Indian Head Pond. It was purchased by Clifford and Jessie Morse in 1946. Their son and his wife, Roland and Marie Morse, run the Indian Head Transportation business from the property today.

Dr. Flavel Thomas of Maquan Street was a very popular doctor in town. He not only delivered a large number of Hanson babies, but as can be see n here, he seems to have published a virtual résumé in this advertisement from the *Hanson Resident and Business Directory* of 1902–1903.

Capt. Joseph Smith purchased this Federal-style home at 149 Maquan Street with the prize money he won in the Revolutionary War. Another owner was Dr. Flavel Thomas, who established his practice in Hanson in 1879. Thomas's wife, Caroline Thomas, was the great-granddaughter of Joseph Smith. Dr. Thomas also opened a sanitorium here in 1894 for the treatment of chronic diseases.

Nathaniel Thomas built his home *c.* 1760 at 527 Liberty Street, at the corner of Winter Street directly opposite the town hall. The house was moved some 300 feet westward in 1930, when the town voted to reconstruct the corner of Liberty and Winter Streets, as ordered by the county commissioners, doing away with the bad corner and improving the town hall grounds. It was demolished in 1968 to allow construction of Ferry's Sunoco gas station. In this 1912 view, the crowd was attending a celebration held across the street at the town hall.

Built *c.* 1760, the Nathaniel Thomas house stood at the corner of Liberty and Winter Streets. The house was moved in 1930, when the town voted to reconstruct the corner. Ferry's Sunoco gas station currently stands on this property.

The house and large barn at 357 Liberty Street was built *c.* 1820 by Charles Howland, who was a carpenter by trade. James McRoberts lived here for many years. Later, the property was owned by Andrew and Martha Kiddey and then by Paul E. Schultz.

The home at 201 Spring Street was built by Eldridge Ramsdell in 1836. The stable was built in 1846. It was later sold to Daniel Lewis, who was a founder and first president of the Hanson Historical Society. Lewis's daughter, Patricia, came into this world in the borning room (a warm room off the kitchen). Patricia Lewis Stearns was a selectwoman in the town of Hanson. Daniel Lewis sold the home to John Anderson, who sold it to Matthew and Carolyn Palermo on November 10, 1971.

Eleazer Hamlin built the house at 131 Holmes Street in the early 1750s and occupied it for nearly 20 years. By 1830, it had become the home of Isaac Lowden, who lived there for over 25 years. Lowden's daughter married Capt. Samuel Briggs, and the couple became the owners of the house in the last quarter of the 19th century and remained there until their deaths. Since then, it has held a succession of owners.

The home at 311 Holmes Street was built by Adolph Banuk, who lived in Quincy. He started construction in the 1940s, building it completely by hand. Banuk finished it in the 1960s and then used it as his summer home.

The Thomas house, at 324 Holmes Street, is a one-and-a-half-story ell house built in the 1770s by Edward Thomas. It was sold 25 years later to T. Perkins, the first of several Perkins family members who owned the house. The house remained in the Perkins family for at least 70 years. In the early 1930s, it was purchased by Stanislaus Banuk. It is shown here after a fire on April 20, 1941. It was later rebuilt.

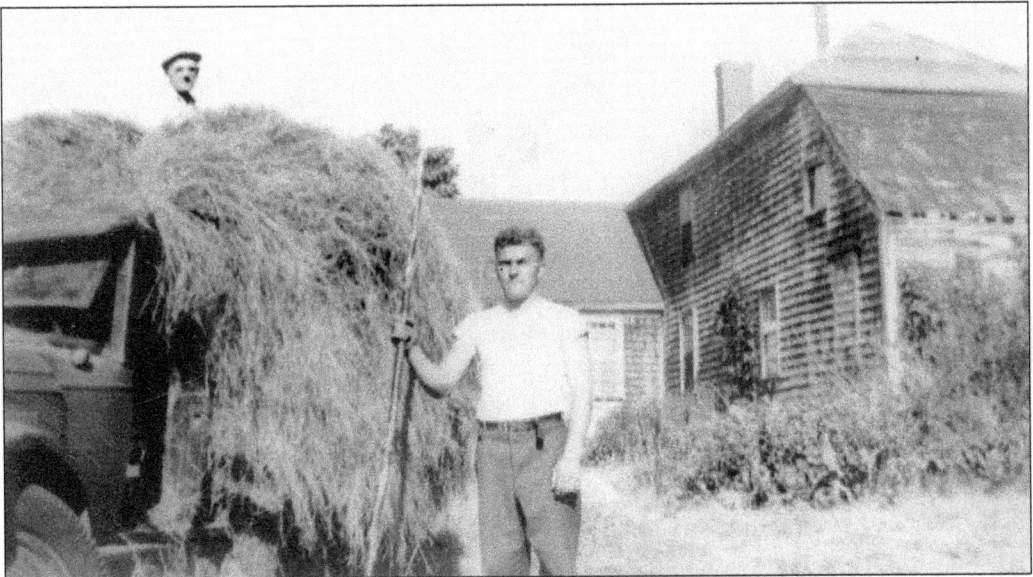

The home at 324 Holmes Street was fairly isolated and surrounded by fields and woods, suggestive of Hanson's 19th-century, rural-agricultural landscape. Shown before the fire are the house, homeowner Stanislaus Banuk (left), and his son, Adolph Banuk, bringing in the hay in the early 1940s.

The Joseph White estate was established in 1833 on West Washington Street. Joseph White sold horses, carriages, wagons, and tack. From left to right are Tuck Wright, Herbert Sprague, and owner Joseph White Jr. in front of the carriage repository, the stable, the office, and another repository (also from left to right). Nothing remains of these buildings today.

The house at 316 West Washington Street was built by Charles Cushing in 1785. Later, the house was owned by his son, Nathaniel Cushing. It remained in the family until the 1930s. Sallie B. Cushing owned it for over 30 years. This 1905 view was quite likely taken from the windmill tower across the street at the Wells Elliott house. Behind the Cushing house was Cushing's Pond, the site of a box factory that was operated by Nathaniel Cushing during the 1800s.

The home of Wells Elliott was located at 271 West Washington Street. This early photograph shows the house before the windmill and outbuildings were added.

This view of the West Washington home of Wells Elliott was taken c. 1910. It shows the numerous additions and outbuildings that were used by Wells Elliott for his various pursuits, which included photography and trolley construction. One of his horse-drawn traveling photographic studios can be seen to the left of the house.

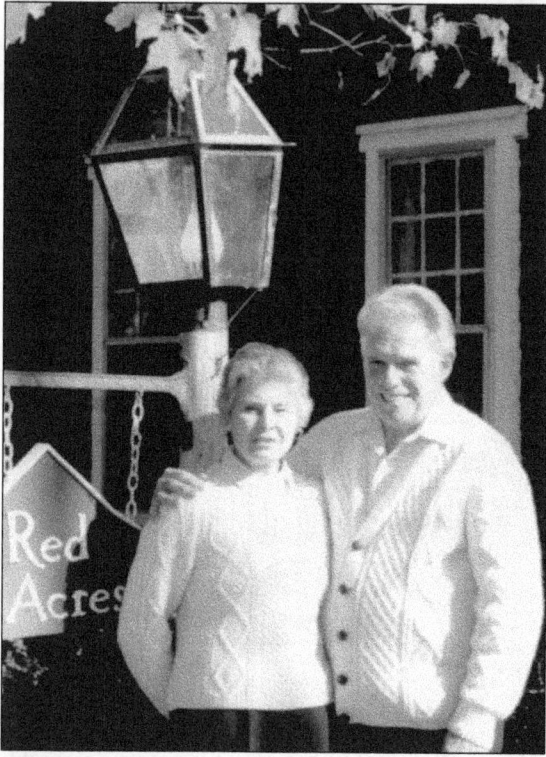

The Red Acres Farm is located at 517 West Washington Street. The owners, Mary and George Mullen, hosted the Red Acres Sing at the holidays for more than 45 years. Three of their children have now built homes on the property.

This is the pre-Revolutionary home of George and Mary Mullen's family. John Beal built the original center-chimney saltbox structure in the 1730s on Willow Street. The house was later called the Drake-Fuller house. Professor Drake ran an antiques and second-hand store on the property. Today, the address is 517 West Washington Street. The Mullen family renamed the property Red Acres and painted all the buildings barn red. From 1950 to 1994, it was a working farm with sheep, chickens, cows, gardens, and orchards. It continues to be the home of the Mullen family.

The Cushing house, a large and stately old Colonial at 89 East Washington Street on Cushing Corner, was built by Elijah Cushing c. 1724 and has had addresses in four towns. It was built on land that over the years was in Bridgewater, Abington (1712), Hanover (1727), Pembroke (1746), and, finally, incorporated Hanson (1820). Cushing's daughter, Mary, married Hingham native Benjamin J. Lincoln in this house on January 15, 1756. Benjamin Lincoln, of the Massachusetts militia, joined the Continental army and served closely under Gen. George Washington during the Revolutionary War as a major general and later as secretary of war.

This mansard-roof Victorian is located at 63 East Washington Street, to the left of the Elijah Cushing house. It was constructed in the mid-1800s for Andrew Bowker, who owned a shop just west of this house. It later became well known as the Cummings residence.

Evie (left) and Mary Drew are out for a bicycle ride in the 1890s. The daughters of Evelina and Cyrus Drew, they resided in the family home at 55 Spring Street. Evie Drew was a bookkeeper, an accomplished historian, and a news correspondent for the *Bryantville News*. Mary Drew served as the town librarian for 30 years. The library was located first at Thomas Hall and later at her home.

Isaac Soper, a farmer, built this Colonial home at 55 Spring Street *c.* 1797. Cyrus Drew, a Hanson merchant, acquired the property in 1857, and various Drew family members lived here for decades. The outbuildings have been variously used as the Cyrus Drew and Son general store and as a library by Thomas Drew's sister, Mary Drew. Now known as the Soper-Drew house, it was conveyed in 1942 to Lepha and George Strathern, who sold it in 1977 to Barbara and Rodney Brunsell.

Thomas Drew, the son of Cyrus Drew, was born in 1845. He began his career as a clerk in his father's dry goods and grocery store, on Willow Street at Harding's Corner. By the 1870s, Cyrus Drew and Son had relocated to the large barn behind the family home on Spring Street. Thomas Drew moved c. 1880 to Hanover and operated Thomas Drew and Company, a general store located on Broadway Street where Myette's store is currently in business. He also became postmaster of South Hanover and was a successful published photographer.

Cyrus and Thomas Drew, father and son, both served in the Civil War. Thomas Drew is shown here later in life in his uniform. He died in 1913.

This house, located at 474 State Street, was a Ramsdell house, which was passed to the Chapmans when Hilda Ramsdell married Luther Chapman. It was in this house that Sumner Allen Chapman was born in 1874. He attended Williams College and then taught at Pembroke High School. Later, he opened law offices in Plymouth and Rockland.

The Chapman house stands at the corner of Washington and New State Streets. The current address is 474 State Street. From left to right are Hosea Hathaway, Cynthia Underwood Hathaway, Estelle Hathaway, Josephine Underwood Chapman, Sumner A. Chapman, Luther W. Chapman, and Josiah Hathaway.

Five
TRANSPORTATION

Lloyd Sumner Josselyn, age 82, had just returned from a bicycle trip to Hingham. The bike had a 52-inch wheel. It was completely nickel plated, ball-bearing equipped, and had a patent brake arrangement. It cost $150. Sumner Josselyn died at age 87 on August 30, 1947.

Before the days of flashing railroad signals, the crossing tender warned approaching traffic of the danger of an oncoming train. Shown in the early 1900s is crossing tender Horace Brown. The South Hanson Railroad station (right) is located at 1120 Main Street. The house (center) was moved to West Washington Street in the 1980s i

The Old Colony Railroad opened with a celebration on November 10, 1845. On the right is the only remaining train station building left in Hanson. On the left is the Wampatuck Hall. Next was the Central House, a boardinghouse and small store run by Alice W. Crocker. The commuter rail reopened on September 29, 1997.

This Old Colony Railroad station was located at the foot of Pleasant Street until lawyer and businessman Albert Cameron Burrage launched an industrial complex of buildings in this area c. 1905. Soon after construction of the site began, this station was replaced with the new, modern Burrage Station.

The Burrage Station was erected c. 1906 by the New York, New Haven and Hartford Railroad on Pleasant Street across the tracks from the Burrage Industrial Complex. The building was constructed of cement bricks, which were furnished free of charge by the Burrage interests. The station was built on modern principles, with a focus on usefulness and as an ornament to this rapidly growing section of Hanson.

The Monponsett Railroad Station was opened and dedicated in August 1905. The dedication exercises consisted of selections by Briggs Orchestra and the address of the evening by Dr. A.A. Klein, president of the Monponsett Improvement Association. Klein was one of the first to build a summer home in Monponsett. This once popular and active railroad station eventually fell victim to the popularity of the automobile and the curtailment of the commuter railroad service, and it was eventually demolished.

This was the first car to run over the electric street railway system, which opened on July 17, 1900. It ran between Whitman and Bryantville, passing through Hanson. Conductor Thomas Nugent and motorman Frank Goddard were in charge. Town officials of Whitman, Hanson, and Pembroke were passengers on this trip. No fare was exacted.

A trolley from the Brockton and Plymouth Street Railway (later renamed the Plymouth and Brockton Street Railway) with a snowplow attachment has gone off the tracks. This photograph was taken looking eastward toward Bryantville Center, and the house on the right is in Pembroke.

This Plymouth and Brockton Street Railway trolley is traveling southward on Spring Street toward Harding's Corner, where Washington Street splits into east and west. The trolley line ran through Hanson from the Whitman line to Bryantville from 1900 to 1925. Chase's Waiting Room and store is the low box-shaped building on the right.

This express car was rebuilt from an eight-bench open car by Wells Elliott, the Brockton and Plymouth Street Railway shop carpenter, at the rear of his home on West Washington Street. The motorman was Curtis Finny, and the conductor was George Howland. The express business was discontinued on March 1, 1915, but the freight business continued for three more years.

Shown here, in the early stages, is a trolley from the Brockton and Plymouth Street Railway under construction at the home of Wells Elliott, at 271 West Washington Street. Wells Elliott was a talented carpenter and builder. It is interesting to note that very early the railway changed its name from the Brockton and Plymouth Street Railway to the Plymouth and Brockton Street Railway.

This "Town of Hanson"–marked steamroller, the hot-tar tanker truck from the Barrett Manufacturing Company of Boston, and laborers work on a road surface in 1908. Fully paved surfaces were scarce on rural routes at this time, but the laying of the mixture of gravel and oily tar was a tedious job that provided some improvement over dusty dirt roads. Although the property of the town of Hanson, the roller is seen here on loan to a road crew on St. George Street in Duxbury. The steamroller was smashed for scrap metal by the highway department c. 1947.

Albert Burrage bought this steam shovel in the early 1900s to dig from Stump Pond to Sammy's Neck—a distance of more than two miles. He removed the peat moss from the swamp and used it for fuel. He used the ditch to float the peat up in barges. He then could control water flowage from the great Stump Pond to his bogs. Al Hammond was the boss of the Portuguese crew digging the canal. From left to right are Norman MacKenzie, Will Thayer, John Ibbitson, and Elton Brown (an engineer and fireman).

Albert Cushing Read was born into an old Hanson family in 1887. He was born in Lyme, New Hampshire, where his father was preaching. The family returned to Hanson the following year, residing in the Barker homestead, at 930 Main Street at the corner of High Street. Read's uncle, Albert S. Barker, is well-known for his work in hydrographics. Barker led an enterprise that charted maps and took soundings around the world. Much of his work has become established fact and has been used in research and textbooks. Inspired by his uncle, Read also planned on making a name for himself. He graduated from high school with honors for brilliant scholarship and became the youngest man ever accepted to the U.S. Naval Academy, where he graduated fourth in his class in 1907. Lieutenant Commander Read piloted the first transatlantic flight while serving in the navy. Admiral Read retired in 1946 and died in 1947. He is buried in Arlington National Cemetery.

Despite adverse weather conditions, the NC-4 flew on to the Azores through miles of thick fog. A serious collision was avoided during the nighttime flight. The NC-4 was one of three navy planes that started the journey. The navy stationed 48 destroyers along the route, but with the fog, the ships did not have much of a role. For most of the journey, the crew flew blind.

The *New York Times* headline on June 1, 1919, spelled out the first successful transatlantic flight of the navy's NC-4 biplane. It was big news; yet when "Lucky Lindy" made his flight, his name became a household word. The only difference was that Charles Lindbergh flew solo and did not make any stops. However, in 1919, Read's flight was front-page news.

The only recognition for Adm. Albert C. Read in Hanson, besides having his plane featured on the back of the town coin, is a small plaque on the grounds of the Hanson Baptist Church. The plaque was dedicated on Armistice Day, November 11, 1976, in memory of Read and his uncle, Adm. Albert S. Barker. At the ceremony, ministers from several local churches took part in honoring these men, including Rev. Robert H. Heigham from the First Congregational Church, Rev. Robert W. Lamson from the First Baptist Church, and Fr. John E. McLaughlin from St. Joseph the Worker.

Hanson Cranland Airport was established as an airfield in 1960. It was used mostly for crop-dusting planes spraying the cranberry bogs. The airport has a single north–south paved runway that is 60 feet wide and 1,840 feet long, long enough to accommodate light twin-engine aircraft. It continues in operation to this day. On the third Sunday of each month, the airport is open to the public when a "fly-in" is held, complete with a pancake breakfast.

Six

ORGANIZATIONS

Gordon Rest was located at the corner of Indian Head and Maquan Streets. It was built in 1802 by Rev. George Barstow, the second pastor of the Hanson Congregational Church. The New England Helping Hand Society purchased the property in 1887, with help from the estate of philanthropist James Gordon. In 1897, the Massachusetts branch of the International Order of the King's Daughters and Sons bought the house and, after expanding to 25 bedrooms, made its mission "to give a vacation to women, children, and working girls." After the place drifted into limited use, its contents were auctioned off and the building was demolished in 1975. Surviving postcards are testimony to many happy vacations enjoyed here. Today, the site is occupied by the Sullivan Funeral Home.

The Grange hall was built by Gilman Whiting on the site of a previous school known as the South Grammar School, which opened in September 1908. On May 12, 1941, the town deeded the property to Hanson Grange Patrons of Husbandry No. 209—organized in 1909—for the sum of $1. The Grange building is located at 782 Main Street, at the corner of Robinson Street.

The Grange youth group was as successful as the adult group. From left to right in this 1947 photograph are the following: (front row) Joline Snow, three unidentified members, Dale Pitman, Beverly Hammond, two unidentified members, and Rosanne Casoli; (middle row) Mary Lavagni, two unidentified members, Roberta Lundberg, Bob Smith, Paul Puddington, three unidentified members, Don Smith, and unidentified; (back row) unidentified, Ethel Coffey, unidentified, Dotti Coffey, Barbara Derby, Joanne Brooks, Anne Close, Eleanor Bates, and Phil Parker.

Theodore Lyman Bonney, for whom the Hanson Grand Army of the Republic (GAR) post was named, was born on October 27, 1836, in Taunton. He moved to Hanson as a young boy. He enlisted on December 2, 1861, and became a sergeant in Company E 1st Massachusetts Infantry Battalion. On April 27, 1863, the army broke camp and moved to Chancellorsville, where it encountered the rebel army. Overcome by exposure and fatigue, Bonney was taken to a field hospital where, sick with typhoid fever, he died on May 11, 1863. He was buried at the Potomac Creek Station. His brother, Otis Bonney, had his remains disinterred and brought to Hanson to be laid to rest in the family plot.

Members of the Theodore L. Bonney Post No. 127 gather together on October 10, 1908. From left to right are the following: (front row) A.L. Dame, G. Beal, C.G. Moore, S.M. Briggs, John Scates, O.L. Bonney, and C. Atwood (standing); (back row) G.F. Ford, N.T. Howland, G.F. Tew, E. Pratt, I. Bourne, H. Goff, J. Willis, and W.W. Hood. The clock and drum shown in this picture are now the property of the Hanson Historical Society.

John Scates was born in 1841. Although occupied by farming, lumbering, and being town clerk for many years, he is most remembered for valiant military service in the Civil War and for his dedicated attention to veterans' affairs. Enlisting in the 1st Massachusetts Infantry in 1861, Scates served in many combat campaigns, including the first Bull Run, Malvern Hill, Wilderness, and Spotsylvania campaigns. Sergeant Scates was mustered out in May 1864. Having joined the GAR in 1870, he served as commander of Hanson's Theodore L. Bonney Post No. 127 for 19 years starting in 1904. As the town's last surviving Civil War veteran, he died in Hanson in 1931.

The Grand Army hall, located on the west side of High Street, was constructed in 1903–1904. It was a gift to the membership of Theodore L. Bonney Post No. 127 GAR by lumber and box magnate John Foster. The deed passed on April 1, 1904, for the sum of $1. The first meeting at the new hall took place on August 12, 1904, with John Scates as commander.

By the 1920s, GAR commander John Scates would open each meeting alone, take up the business of each chair and close the meeting by himself, thus keeping alive the memory of those who served. In 1923, Scates was forced to give up the charter of the post when he had outlived every other member save one invalid, Joseph Clemons. Today, this building is divided into four apartments.

SECOND GRAND
HURDY-GURDY PARTY

AT

WAMPATUCK HALL, So. Hanson,

FRIDAY EVENING, MARCH 4, 1898

UNDER AUSPICES OF W. L. A.

Music by the Celebrated Tambourinist,
MARIE GROSSE, with Special HURDY-GURDY.

FLOOR DIRECTOR - - LESTER CHAMBERLAIN.
AIDS - - R. C. EVERSON, A. C. SAMPSON.

COMMITTEE OF ARRANGEMENTS:
J. E. Josselyn, A. C. Sampson, W. L. Chamberlain, R. C. Everson,
Alice Keene, Ella F. Brown, M. Ella Ford, Alice Crocker.

TICKETS ADMITTING GENT AND ONE LADY, **50 CTS.** Extra Lady, 25c.

Refreshments served in Lower Hall.   Dancing from 8 till 1.

THE ABOVE CELEBRATED CHAMPION TAMBOURINE PLAYER WILL
POSITIVELY APPEAR AT THIS PARTY.

So, what was this music at Wampatuck Hall in 1898? Webster's definition of hurdy-gurdy is "a. A musical instrument, shaped like a lute, whose strings are set in vibration by the edge of a wheel turned by a crank. b. Any musical instrument, as a hand organ, played by turning a handle." To get the full effect of the hurdy-gurdy and tambourine, as they say, you had to be there.

Wampatuck Hall, located at 1131 Main Street, was dedicated on November 18, 1893. Formerly a library built by the Little Workers Sewing Circle, the library was on the first floor and there was a hall on the second floor. Many functions were held here: potluck suppers, dances, whist parties, and minstrel shows. The building was leased to the Wampatuck Lodge A.F. & A.M. on May 29, 1946. Today, it houses a day-care center.

The American Legion Hall was purchased on August 3, 1935, from the Rockland Savings Bank for $835.07. It was formerly the Floette Tea Room, on the corner of Crooker Place and Main Street. The Legion had the building moved to Robinson Street on land given to them by the United Cape Cod Cranberry Company through the courtesy of Marcus Urann.

Boy Scout Troop No. 1 from Hanson gathers for a picture in 1929. From left to right are Allan Shepherd, unidentified, Frank Meinhold, Ken MacKenzie, Carl Meinhold, Edgar Faelten, Calvin Howland, Dick Black, George Anthony, Donald MacSween, Wilfred Reid, Danny Sullivan, Lyman Smith, unidentified, Torchy Hathaway, and Bob Black (scoutmaster).

The Hanson Girl Scouts started in 1918, and Brownie troops started in 1932. Dorothy Campbell (center) was president of the Scouts from 1948 to 1952. By that time, the meetings were held in the parish hall of the Congregational church. Standing with Dorothy Campbell, from left to right, are Sandra MacLellan, Judith Reid, Joan Campbell, and Norma MacLellan.

A Girl Scout rally was held in the Congregational church's parish hall and was attended by parents, friends, and a large delegation from the Hanson Boy Scouts. The event was the awarding of the curved bars, the highest honor of Girl Scouts, by Dorothy Campbell (right). From left to right are Mrs. William Hopkins (troop leader), Nancy Hokanson, Deborah Baker, Margaret Nice, and Dorothy Davis.

Seven

COMMERCE AND INDUSTRY

One of South Hanson's earliest industries was cedar logging, as seen in this photograph of the great cedar swamp. Used for posts, rails, and shingles, cedar also played an important part in the shipbuilding industry by supplying timber.

Captain Moore's Sawmill was built in the early 1700s and was located near Poor Meadow River on West Washington Street. The mill was originally a forge built and operated by Theodosius Moore soon after he bought the land in 1704. The pond bore the name of Moore's Pond and is now known as Forge Pond.

John Ibbitson is shown on his wagon with his team of four horses. He has a shipment of box boards for delivery. This picture was taken on Elm Street across from the Ibbitson home.

In 1850, Edward Y. Perry of Hanson, Ezra Phillips of Hanover, and Martin Stetson of Hanover formed a partnership under the name of E.Y. Perry & Company for the purpose of manufacturing tacks. This sprawling factory with its various additions was located on the Hanson-Hanover line on State Street. By 1874, Stetson and Perry were retired and the business continued under the name Ezra Phillips & Sons Tack Works. The firm thrived for well over a half century. However, nothing remains of the buildings shown in this c. 1905 photograph.

Thomas Mill, across from Wampatuck Pond on Liberty Street, is one of Hanson's earliest building sites. Col. Nathaniel Thomas either received 250 acres in payment for surveying the Major's Purchase tract or bought land from local Native Americans. In 1695, Thomas completed the first dam in Plymouth County for powering a waterwheel. The Thomas family operated the mill until 1829. The building shown here burned in the 1920s. Hanson's 1976 bicentennial project volunteers launched a new mill construction project shepherded by Frank Sawyer Sr. The waterwheel was designed and its creation was supervised by Frank Sawyer Jr.

Well-known Hanson merchant John Foster was born in 1842 into a Pembroke family. He began his business career as a grocer in Pembroke. He moved to Hanson in 1879 and purchased Barnabas Everson's sawmill on Main Street. By the 1890s, he was a major dealer in pine and cedar lumber, cranberry barrels, packing boxes, and excelsior. For 35 years, the John Foster Company supplied wooden packing cases to the Walter Baker Chocolate Company of Dorchester. Foster acquired much real estate and several cranberry bogs in town. He built the GAR hall on High Street and donated it to the Civil War veterans. His company lived on for decades after he died at the age of 67 in 1909.

This invoice from the John Foster Company shows a sale to Abner W. Jackson, a carpenter living in neighboring Whitman. It is for a substantial purchase of building materials in the spring of 1904. Foster's business transactions crossed many town and city boundaries.

In 1898, Frank Keene built Edwin T. Clark's new general store on Main Street facing Phillips Street. Soon after 1900, Edwin Clark retired and his son George Clark ran the business. Later another son, Harold T. Clark, took over as proprietor and operated the store for over half a century. Roger Clark became a third-generation storekeeper. From left to right in this 1912 photograph are store clerks Hollis W. Ibbitson, A. Stanley Gorham, Harold T. Clark, Elbert Munroe, and Clarence Pratt.

One of the most popular bus stops in town was located right in front of the E.T. Clark's store. Waiting for the bus in this photograph, from left to right, are the following: (front row) Nancy George, Carole McNamara, Carole Shea, Rosanne Casoli, and Beverly Hammond; (back row) unidentified, Wilson Brooks, Jackie Mansfield, unidentified, Raymond Reid, and unidentified.

After having operated his business at Soper's Hall, dry goods and furniture merchant Cyrus Drew relocated to this new store in 1868. This c. 1870 view shows where East and West Washington Streets meet, formerly Willow Street, opposite Spring Street. The popular retail spot hosted many merchants through the years. Elmer Loring took over this location when Drew moved his business to his home on Spring Street.

This intersection, shown here c. 1895, became known as Harding's Corner when Henry B. Harding sold dry goods and groceries in the store on the right while also serving as Hanson's postmaster. Harry Holbrook followed in the same business and was also postmaster. Gordon Grant was a mid-20th-century proprietor here, and finally, the Hanson Public Market was in business at this location when fire destroyed the store in 1969. Also gone is the building on the left, Soper's Hall, where town meetings were held before the town hall was built. It was used in the 1860s by merchants Jeremiah Soper, Cyrus Drew, and Andrew Bowker.

Here is a listing of offerings from the Hanson Public Market, on Washington Street at Spring Street, during a December weekend special in 1941. While the prices seem unbelievable by today's standards, it must be remembered that the Great Depression had recently ended and household incomes were a mere fraction of what they are today.

HANSON PUBLIC MARKET

HARDING'S CORNER   TEL., WHITMAN 94-M

WEEK END SPECIALS, DEC. 11, 12 & 13

SUGAR	BACON	BUTTER
10 POUND SACK 59c	POUND 29c	1 POUND ROLL 39c

Deviled Meat	2 For 9c
Bonex Dog Food	3 For 25c
Matchless Shrimp Large Size	23c
Horticultural Beans No. 2 Can	15c
Concentrated Super Suds	2 For 35c
Asparagus No. 2 Can	29c
Fresh Cucumber Pickles Quart	25c
Crispy Rings	25c
Windex	15c
Cando Silver Polish	25c
Junket Freezing Mix	3 For 25c
Argo Gloss Starch	2 For 19c
O'Cedar Furniture Polish	25c
Soy Sauce	10c

Fruits and Vegetables

Oranges	2 Dozen 39c
Grapefruit	4 For 25c
Apples Baldwins	5 Pounds 25c
Cucumbers	Each 10c
Turnips	Pound 4c
Cabbage	Pound 4c
Pascal Celery	22c

Quality Meats

Sausage	Pound 33c
Sausage Meat	Pound 33c
Sirloin Roll	Pound 39c
Sliced Bacon	Pound 29c
Frankforts	Pound 23c
Ham Shanks	Pound 15c
Corned Beef	Pound 32c

Tomatoes	Evaporated Milk	FLORIDA ORANGES
2 No. 2 CANS 23c	3 TALL CANS 25c	2 DOZEN 39c

FRESH FISH THURSDAYS & FRIDAYS
FREE DELIVERY

W.W. Copeland Grain and Coal Company was situated on West Washington Street near the railroad tracks. The Copelands lived on the second floor of their company. To the right of the company were the grain, hay, and coal sheds. The business burned on October 18, 1906. The fire was set from sparks from the engine of the 6:36 train. The building on the south side of the tracks housed the North Hanson post office, general store, waiting room, and freight office. Hanson Grain is now located here.

SIDNEY E. FORD,

LIVERY AND BOARDING STABLES

Large or Small Parties Accommodated at Any Time.

AGENT FOR

New York and Boston Despatch Express.

Express leaves So. Hanson at 7
A. M. for Bryantville, Hanson
Centre and No. Hanson, connecting with the 10.22 A. M. train
for Boston.

Stable and Office, Main Street, opp. the Depot,

This advertisement from the *Hanson Resident and Business Directory* of 1906 shows how dependent we were on the horse at a time when the automobile was just emerging in the big cities but still only a curiosity in rural America. Sidney Ford not only provided customers transportation by coach but also performed cargo services, including moving furniture or pianos.

Ford's Livery Stable, seen here in 1912, was located at 1125 Main Street. Sidney E. Ford ran a livery and boarding stable opposite the South Hanson depot. Notice both automobile and horse and wagon are included in this photograph. It is currently operating as Cyclops Power Equipment Company. Shown next on the right is the Wampatuck Hall.

This 1907 handbill announces Frank Goff's shoe store opening on Pleasant Street near Reed Street in South Hanson. Frank Goff's home was on the same property. The printed dates indicate a five-day period for getting this important message out before the grand opening. The Goff Shoe Store remained open for 44 years.

GRAND OPENING!

The subscriber wishes to inform the Public, that he will open his new

SHOE STORE

| On Pleasant Street, South Hanson. | | On Monday Evening, June 10, 1907. |

I shall have a full line of
MENS, WOMENS, BOYS AND YOUTHS SHOES.
Also Special Agent for
WHITCOMB'S FLEXOLE LADIES SHOES.
I shall also have on sale
Several Cases of Slightly Damaged Shoes,
AT LOW PRICES.

A box of BLACKING and a SHOE HORN, given with each sale made on the opening evening.

A good Cobbler connected with the store.

Having located in Cushing Corner at 16 Liberty Street, Edward Cox launched his restaurant and bar in the early 1930s. This haven for food, beverages, and frequent live musical entertainment served Hanson patrons for about 20 years before Cox's untimely death in the early 1950s. For the next couple of decades, this location served as Jeff's Restaurant and then was succeeded by the current establishment, J.J.'s Pub, a favorite spot in town for the past 30 years.

The Atlantic Dye Company plant was built on Hawkes Avenue, a part of the Burrage industries. It was ravaged by fire on March 6, 1919. This picture was taken from one of the upstairs rooms of the Crest Hotel, at 350 Pleasant Street. The plant and the hotel were both part of the section of Hanson called Burrage.

Built of cement blocks in 1907 on the west side of Pleasant Street during the early days of the Burrage industrial complex, the Crest Hotel had 22 rooms, a lobby, and business meeting rooms. After the Dye works explosion of 1919, and with much of the industrial complex idle, there was no longer a need for a hotel. The Crest Hotel was later demolished by a Brockton wrecking firm and taken away piece by piece. Only the steps remain at the home on this property at 350 Pleasant Street.

The Wheeler Reflector Company, a division of Franklin Research Corporation, was founded in 1881. It is the oldest American lighting company. It was instrumental in the design and development of efficient lighting fixtures from the early gas and oil lamps to the modern industrial and commercial fixtures of today. The company was located on Hawkes Avenue and relocated in the 1970s to another part of Massachusetts.

The original buildings in this photograph were owned by A.C. Burrage and Company. The building to the east was the Eastern Tinfoil Company, which manufactured tinfoil. The building to the west was used for cedar-box manufacturing. By the early 1900s, both buildings were owned by the Wheeler Reflector Company. Lite Control purchased the buildings and land in the early 1970s and continues operating to this day.

Wells Elliott, a famous Hanson photographer, used this photograph wagon as a traveling business studio. His specialty was fine tintypes. This picture was taken in 1892 at the Bridgewater Fairgrounds. The driver was Fred Cushing.

On the side of this 1892 wagon was written "Photograph and Ferrotype Car." This photograph was taken in front of Sagamore Hill at Nantasket. The horses belonged to Otis Cushing of Weymouth. This is one of many portable photographic wagons built and owned by photographer Wells Elliott.

Wells Elliott is shown building one of his portable photograph wagons. Elliott was a steam printer for Jordan Marsh Company in Boston and built rail cars before starting a career in photography. His crime collection photographs included the only picture of Lizzie Borden's father after his death and pictures from the Sturtevant murder in Halifax. A total of 50 glass negatives taken by Wells Elliott are part of the Stonehill College collection.

North Hanson, Mass., _____ 187_

M__

To W. S. ELLIOTT, Jr.

MANUFACTURER OF AND DEALER IN

PICTURE FRAMES OF ALL DESCRIPTIONS.

PARTICULAR ATTENTION GIVEN TO FRAMING SOLDIER'S DIPLOMAS, AND LARGE PICTURES OF ALL KINDS.

Orders by Mail, or otherwise, will receive prompt attention.

W. S. ELLIOTT,

CARPENTER & BUILDER,

HANSON, MASS.

Lock Box 18.

JOBBING PROMPTLY ATTENDED TO.

75 3

Please PAY for this CHECK when PRESENTED.

Price 75c.   No. in Group 3.

GOOD

For 3 Tintypes.

Give this Check to the Operator.

As the billhead, business card, and the "good for" card attest, Wells Elliott of North Hanson was a very talented and busy merchant. He took many of the photographs used in this book.

Jennie Dame purchased this small business from Mrs. Andrew Reed in the early 1900s. She soon added a new wing and began to sell newspapers and magazines and other small items. She died suddenly in 1912, and her husband, Albert Dame, and her sister ran the business until 1918. William Walkey purchased the business on March 3, 1918, and enlarged it several times. Located on Liberty Street at the corner of County Road, it became the site of Walkey's Supermarket.

William Walkey succeeded Dame's Waiting Room at this 470 Liberty Street address. Walkey's small general store and Socony filling station is shown here c. 1930. Later, Walkey became a major retail grocer by expanding into a modern market and adding a liquor store. The business thrived for decades at this location, continuing under the management of his son, W. Robert Walkey. Currently, this site is home to 14-58 Liquors. For many years, the Walkey family lived in the historic Hitchcock house, on High Street, a short walk from the business.

This photograph shows Wilkie's camps and store as they appeared c. 1920. At this location, on Maquan Street at the edge of Maquan Lake, the thirsty patron could get a drink at the bar or the hungry Hansonian could relax lakeside and enjoy such offerings as sandwiches, pastries, Goulding's Spring Tonic, fruit, candy, and tobacco.

The rear view of Wilkie's shows some of the camps and the store. Seven cottages on or near Maquan Lake were available to rent. By the 1960s, the business had wound down. The principal building is now a private home.

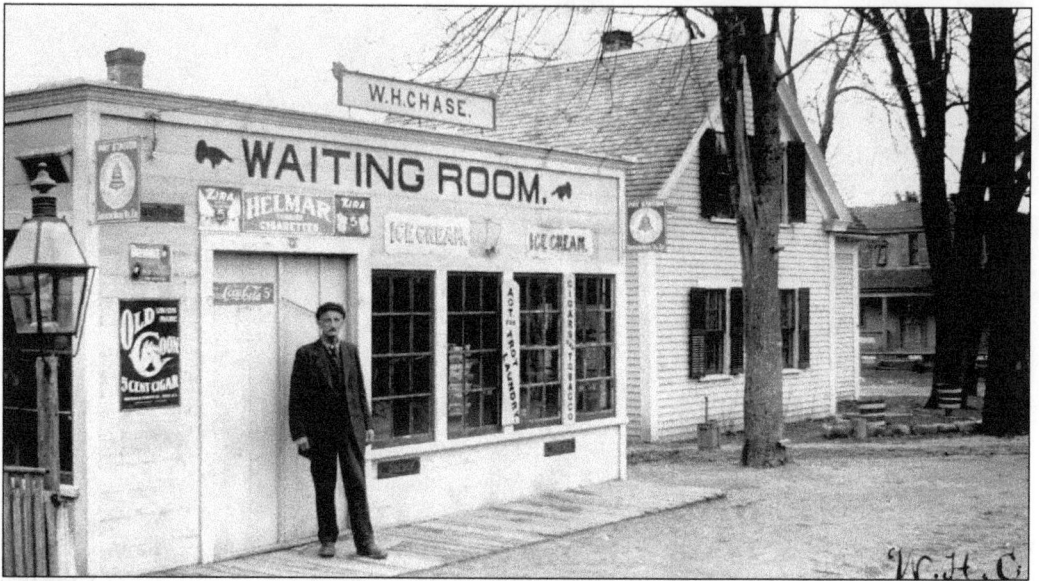

In 1900, the arrival of the Plymouth and Brockton Street Railway trolley line to Hanson coincided with Charles Ramsdell opening this business, located on Spring Street near Harding's Corner, where East and West Washington Streets meet. Customers could eat and smoke products purchased at the waiting room until the trolley arrived. Walter H. Chase purchased the store in 1912 and offered ice cream, confectionary, canned goods, cigars, and tobacco. The business was discontinued in 1925, when the trolley line was eliminated, and the building was removed in 1927.

The original brick building on Main Street was built by Marr Brothers & Stewart of Boston in 1910 for Dr. Myron L. Marr. James M. Bourne did the woodwork, and later the annex building, for the Friend brothers, owners of Friends Beans of Melrose. Marcus Urann formed the United Cape Cod Cranberry Company in 1906, and soon after, purchased this building to use as the central packing house. Later named Ocean Spray Cranberry Company, the business is now located in Middleboro-Lakeville.

Marcus Urann was born in 1873 in Maine. He received his undergraduate degree at the University of Maine, graduated from the Boston University School of Law, and practiced law in Easton. Introduced to the profit potential of cranberries by a client, he purchased his first bog in Halifax in 1906. He formed the United Cape Cod Cranberry Company in 1906 and thereafter established a centralized plant for screening, grading, sorting, packing, and shipping cranberries. In 1930, Urann was the primary force behind an effort to merge three of the largest cranberry canners: himself, Makepeace of Barnstable, and Elizabeth Lee of New Jersey. This new organization was first known as Cranberry Canners, next as National Cranberry, and finally, as Ocean Spray Cranberry Company. After a very successful career, Urann retired in 1953. He died in 1963, but is remembered as a cranberry entrepreneur who revolutionized the industry in Hanson and throughout the United States by the canning of cranberries and the formation of the Ocean Spray Cranberry Company.

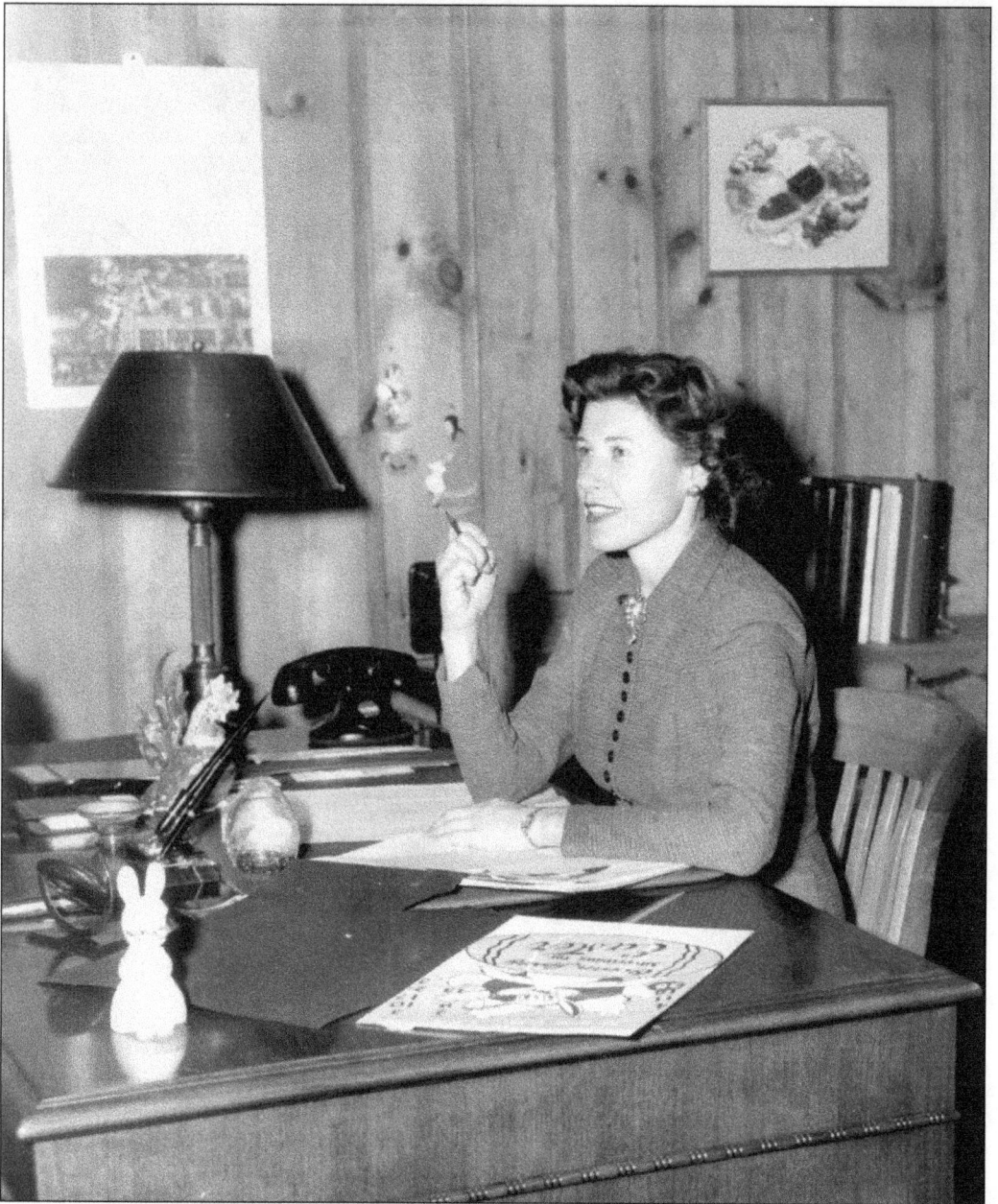

Ellen Stillman is shown at her desk at the Ocean Spray Cranberry Company. In 1932, she began her career at the company, which was then called Cranberry Canners. In time, she moved from the mail room to the advertising department and soon became the advertising manager. One of her first decisions was to install a test kitchen. She wrote a script of cranberry news for company founder Marcus Urann to broadcast over the radio to growers. In 1947, she launched a campaign to link chicken with cranberry sauce. She eventually was promoted to vice president. In 1956, she left the Ocean Spray Cranberry Company to become vice president of Herman W. Stevens, an advertising agency. In 1971, Houghton Mifflin published her *Ski Country Cookbook*. Today, she continues to supervise the bogs her father cultivated in the mid-1940s. She still lives on Elm Street, where her family has lived since 1919.

Shown working a local bog in 1961 are Joanne and Walter Estes, their children—Cathy, Debbie, and Laurie—and a friend who helped with the work. Estes is using a mechanical harvester that combs the berries from the vines.

At this Hanson bog, the work force included not only local town members but also many members of the local Cape Verdean population. All of the cranberries were still being picked with a cranberry scoop when this photograph was taken. The cranberry pickers' work helped to make the cranberry industry very successful.

The *Ocean Spray-er*, the first helicopter purchased by the Ocean Spray Cranberry Company, was used to dust the crops. From left to right are Marcus Urann, Red Roelofs, and Slim Soule. The picture was taken in June 1947.

Marcus Urann's Christmas party at the Ocean Spray Cranberry Company plant was the highlight of the 1951 holiday season in Hanson, and all were welcome to attend. From left to right are the following: (front row) Charles Brine, Marion Goodwin, Alice Larnsworth, George Kay, Lee Meinhold, and unidentified; (middle row) Gail Glover, Glenn Brooks, Marilyn Meinhold, Tom Smith, Linda Meinhold, Suzanne Smith, Beverly Heigham, and Joanne Brooks (Urann's granddaughter); (back row) James Glover, Ruth Brooks (Urann's only daughter), Marcus Urann, and Santa Claus. At the party, the children were treated to a small toy from Santa, a dish of ice cream, and a movie.

100

The ell of the house located at 4 West Washington Street was dragged from Bonney Hill for the widow Taylor, who occupied it until her death. It changed hands several times, first belonging to Reverend Wales and then to Martin Beal, who made coffins. Next, it belonged to Joseph B. White, whose grandson Harold Churchill was the next owner. Churchill's wife, Nan, had a gift shop. It has been home to George and Marjorie Leighton and the Leighton Funeral Home since 1976. In 2003, it became the Leighton-McKinnon Funeral Home.

In 1934, Eddie Johnson bought a home on Spring Street. He had the henhouse moved closer to the road and named it the Chicken Coop. In 1946, Thomas and Beatrice Keefe bought the place and changed the name to the Hitching Post. The business at 48 Spring Street was sold in 1961 to Lyle and Grace Waite, in 1965 to Clifford Rogers and Margaret Farrell, and in 1984 to Arthur and Joan Leanos, who named it the Olde Hitching Post and opened it as a restaurant. The place continues to be one of the finest restaurants in Hanson today.

This 1934 photograph shows the stately home at 930 Main Street, at the corner of High Street. The house was built 100 years earlier by Joseph Barker, father of the later occupant, Adm. Albert Barker. When prominent businessman and call firefighter Alvin Reid lived here, he rented the Butterfield family a stand that dispensed Vita-Cream ice cream. The stand moved to Main Street at Phillips Street, becoming Reid's insurance agency. The Butterfields moved their business to Rockland, where it flourishes today. The house did not survive.

Simeon Thompson bought this building in 1915 for use in connection with his coal business. At that time, the building was located between Clark's store and the Ocean Spray Cranberry Company building. In 1929, Thompson sold the building to Norman MacDonald, who had it moved to 1158 Main Street. In 1947, MacDonald sold the gas station to his brother-in-law Lloyd Prario. Since 1982, Prario's son Clayton has been operating the business.

This is a view from the air of the MacDonald Fuel Corporation, which was owned and operated by Norman MacDonald. In the 1940s, MacDonald expanded the business to include coal and oil. At the time of his death, the company was sold to Hanson Fuel. The station in the front also belonged to Norman MacDonald at one time.

This political postcard dated September 8, 1950, was sent out by Norman G. MacDonald when he was running for the office of county commissioner. Printed on the back of the card was the following: "Norman G. MacDonald, Pres. & Treas. of MacDonald Fuel Corp., Director of Rockland Trust Co., Trustee Whitman Savings Bank, Chairman Hanson School Comm., Former Selectman, Past Pres. Ply. County Rep. Club, would appreciate your support and vote at the Primaries, September 19th." He won the election.

John Ferry is shown receiving an award from Jenney Oil Company executives in recognition of high sales of gasoline. John's Jenney station was located at 203 Liberty Street and later renamed John's Citgo. In 1974, it moved to a new location at 527 Liberty Street. It is currently Ferry's Sunoco station.

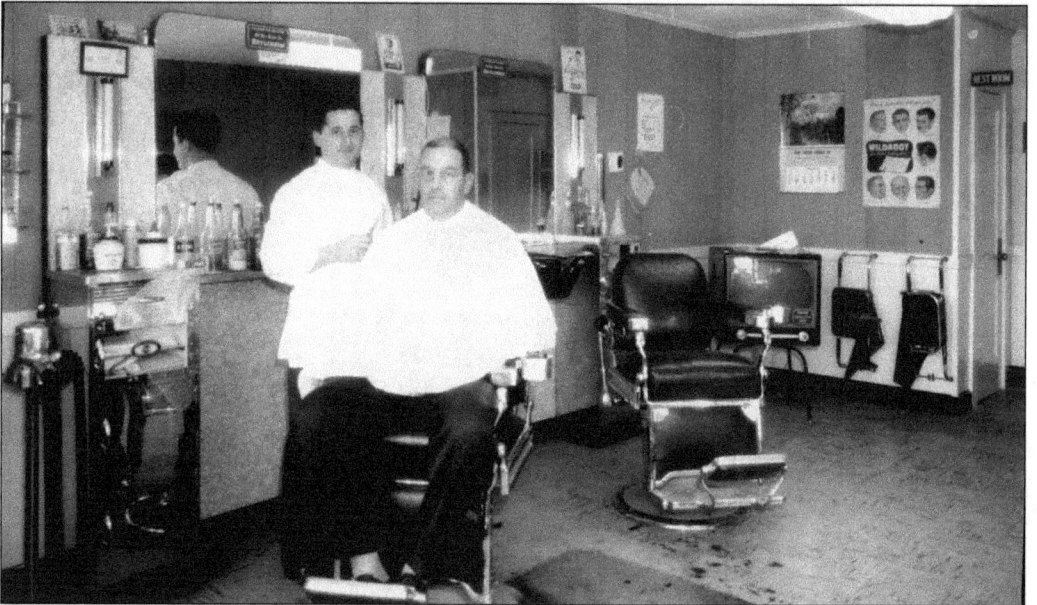

Don Botieri started his career as a barber in the town of Hanson in 1950. He is best known as "Mr. Baseball," serving Hanson Little League for over 25 years as cofounder, coach, and eventually Little League president. He lives on High Street with his wife of 50 years, Betty. At age 74, he continues to work at his barbershop and has no plans to retire. He says he likes to be remembered as one of the "Burrage boys," having grown up in the section of South Hanson near Burrage Pond.

Eight

CELEBRATIONS AND LEISURE

Hanson sportsmen pose after hunting geese *c.* 1910 on Fern Island in Wampatuck Pond behind the town hall. From left to right, the successful hunters are Frank Baker, Roderick McClellan, and Charles Moore and his son Leslie Moore.

The South Hanson Brass Band was organized and directed by Seth Miller Briggs. Band members' uniforms were bought with contributions and dance and concert money. Shown on the town hall steps in this 1880 photograph are, from left to right, the following: (front row) Seth Miller Briggs (leader), Otis Hood, Frank Goff, Charles Ford, Everett Josselyn, Charles Selon, George Hammond, Joshua Bowles Hammond, and Joshua Wilson Hammond; (back row) Frank Hammond, Elmer Johnson, Walter Calder, Dr. Samuel Howland, Thomas Fuller, Oscar Johnson, Webb Dow, Albert Josselyn, Edgar Josselyn, and Isaac Bourne.

The South Hanson Brass Band gathers in 1880 in front of Seth Miller Briggs's house, on Pleasant Street, where they practiced. From left to right are the following: (front row) George A. Hammond, Otis Hood, Joshua B. Hammond, Joshua W. Hammond, Dr. Samuel Howland, and Frank Hammond; (middle row) unidentified, Charles Selon, Everett Josselyn, Oscar Johnson, Frank Goff, Walter Calder, Elmer Johnson, Edgar Josselyn, and unidentified; (back row) Elliot Thrasher, Isaac Bourne, and Albert Josselyn.

106

Seth Miller Briggs is shown with his violin. He could be found any day in his workshop next to his home on Pleasant Street in South Hanson. He made and repaired violins and was the leader of the Briggs orchestra. He also repaired clocks, taught music, was a dancing master, tuned organs and pianos, was a woodworker, wrote music, and was a licensed auctioneer. His musical ability was fondly remembered by his comrades in the Union service in 1862.

In 1886, Jessie Alton Lewis organized 21 Hanson ladies into the first all-female brass band in New England. Seth Turner was the band's first instructor, succeeded by Thomas Fuller. From left to right are the following: (front row) Carrie Milward Briggs, Annie Poole Atwood, Mary Barrows, Idella Arnold, Ida Raymond, Augusta Ramsdell, and Francella Bowker; (back row) Elva Turner, Mary Foster Fuller, Julie Poole, Jessie Lewis, Georgia Josselyn, Thomas Fuller (instructor), Mamie Wheeler, and Leona Corbin.

This is the Burrage baseball team in 1910. The team played on Burrage Field, which is on the corner of Main and Pleasant Streets. The uniforms were maroon with white lettering. From left to right are the following: (front row) Herman Thomas and Sherman McClellan; (middle row) Roderick McClellan, Harry Tucker, Harold Clark, Merton Howard, and William Dunham; (back row) Burton Shepherd, James Lowery, Edwin Churchill (umpire), and Adolphus Beal. Marcus Urann is sitting in his touring car on the right.

This 1939 photograph shows the league champions, the Hanson Canners Plymouth County and Old Colony baseball team. From left to right are the following: (front row) Tony Spath (captain), Tony Correa, Kenneth "Mac" MacKenzie, "Allie" Chamberlain, and Tony Pignatelli; (back row) Bill Darsch, John Quinlan, Frank "Wink" Gardner, Cliff "Red" McNamara, Fred "Rick" Verdone, Frank Swanson, and George Sayce. Missing from picture is "Al" Trosky.

108

This was the summer home of Albert Burrage, a wealthy Boston attorney, copper baron, and industrialist. He built his summer home in 1905 and named it the Needles. It was located on the southeast side of Maquan Pond among 64 acres of pines, oaks, and rhododendrons, and it was the pride of Albert Burrage. It was totally destroyed by fire, including the household furniture, clothing, jewels, and cash. All members of the household escaped. The man shown would have been part of the Burrage staff. Albert Burrage rebuilt his beloved Needles.

The Needles has a large wraparound porch overlooking the pristine waters of Maquan Pond. Shown are two boys, one sitting in a chair carved into a large tree. The Needles was rebuilt after a fire, and the porch is as beautiful today as it appears in this picture.

This very rustic shelter was not connected to the Needles but sat off to the side. In the middle of this shelter was another large tree stump.

A group of businessmen poses for a picture on the grounds of the Needles. This photograph was taken in the early 1900s.

In 1922, Albert Burrage sold his summer home, the Needles, to the Boston Camp Fire Girls. The purchase price was $25,000. The Kiwanis International of Boston donated $24,000, and the last $1,000 was donated by Burrage himself. The Camp Fire Girls renamed it Camp Kiwanis and used the estate as a summer camp and retreat. In 1961, they built additional cabins and attendant buildings and expanded the lodge with the construction of the dining hall, which also served as an auditorium.

Camp Kiwanis opened on July 25, 1923, with the arrival of 250 girls. The most popular camp feature was the water toboggan slide. The girls slept in army tents without floors. In 1930, Camp Kiwanis was able to advertise the accommodations of two cabins and 50 tents. Camp Kiwanis continued to expand as time passed, and it housed other organizations, including the American Red Cross. Shown here is the camp store in the late 1930s.

CAMP
KIWANIS

SOUTH HANSON
Plymouth County
MASSACHUSETTS

OUR VIEW OF MAQUAN LAKE

Camp Kiwanis was settled into 50 acres of pine forest. It sat 50 feet above Lake Maquan. The large bungalow has broad verandas on four sides, three open fireplaces, a piano, a reading room, a playroom, and two open-air dining porches. The camp was divided into four villages: Omiske, Yoki, Sheewan, and Wihinapa. In 1957, the Camp Fire Girls officially changed the camp name to Camp Kiwanee, which means "spirit of joy and youth."

Camp Kiwanee, a perfect place for a summer camp, was located on Maquan Pond. Because Maquan Pond had a sandy bottom, the water was crystal clear and ideal for swimming. The camp had a 60-foot water toboggan for experienced swimmers and 180 feet of floating piers with diving boards. Swimming instruction and safety on the waterfront were the very best.

112

In 1935, the American Red Cross started to hold its national aquatic training school at Camp Kiwanis. Shown on the edge of the Maquan Pond is a 1946 group of the American Red Cross.

On July 31, 1979, the town of Hanson purchased Camp Kiwanee from the Council for Greater Boston Camp Fire Girls for $185,000. The Needles Lodge at Camp Kiwanee has a wide wraparound porch overlooking Maquan Pond. The lodge has a capacity for 200 people and a commercial kitchen with walk-in refrigerator. Here, many town activities have taken place, including wedding receptions, theatrical productions, and Hanson Scout troop sleepovers.

Camp Kiwanee has hosted a variety of functions. On June 17, 1989, the girls held a tea party. From left to right are Ellen Galambos, Lauren Fish, Joanne Blauss, Heather Howland, Whitney Blake, Edna Howland, Cindy Fish, Emily Richter, Kathy Baker, Sharon Troupe, and Meghan Richter. The antique dress collection belonged to Phyllis Keith.

Drama continues to this day at Camp Kiwanee. Here is the cast of *End of the Season*, a play directed by Wes Blauss in September 1987. From left to right, the members of cast are as follows: (first row) Pat Flanagan, Jerri Walsh, Scott Kitchenham, Heather Howland, and Lenore Del Grazzo; (second row) Barbara Seamans, Ruth Stoddard, Mark Fish, Fran Kneeland, Sharon Troupe, Peggy Kitchenham, Chris Kitchenham, Eric Martin, Tom Long, Cindy Fish, and Nathaniel Blauss; (third row) Ede Mitchell, Al Galambos, Marty Craven, Ray Fish, Kathy Mitchell, Carolyn Galambos, Edna Howland, John Seamans, Lauren Fish, Maria ? (an exchange student), Ellen Galambos, Barbara Tirrell, and Joanne Blauss; (fourth row) Jim Kneeland and Wes Blauss.

114

Administration Building
New dining porch-left

Rainbow Camp is located at 526 Indian Head Street. Rainbow Camp was founded in 1948 by Lulu H. Gobrecht, the founder of Rainbow Assemblies in Massachusetts. This picture of the main building was taken in 1953. The Rainbow Camp continues to welcome Rainbow campers to this day.

This stone fireplace is inside the main administration building and looks just as it did in this 1953 photograph. Not shown in this photograph is a box that now sits in front of the fireplace that reads, "Sears Poultry Farm, Indian Head Street, South Hanson, Mass.," a souvenir of the former owners.

Rear Administration
building-Infirmary-
Recreation building.

Rainbow Camp was a very active camp in 1953, when this picture was taken. Shown here is the rear of the administration building, the infirmary, and the recreation building. Rainbow girls came from all over the state to attend for two weeks at a time.

Rainbow Camp continues to have an excellent swimming and boating program on Maquan Pond. The campers also enjoy riflery, archery, sports, and arts and crafts. This 1953 photograph also has another view of some of their cabins. The camp now holds three one-week sessions.

Rainbow Camp is located on a beautiful cove of Maquan Pond, with acres of shade trees and pines. Campers are housed in cabins, as seen in this 1953 picture.

SECOND CAMPING PERIOD--1960

Divided into four two-week sessions, the camp was very busy in 1960. The author of this book is in the second row at the far right. She was a member of the Wessagussett chapter of Rainbow Girls from South Weymouth. She attended the camp with her cousin, Barbara Cheney, who is third from the right in the second row.

Camp Wampatuck was located on the shore of Lake Wampatuck, or Wampatuck Pond. The camp was established by the Massachusetts branch of the International Order of the King's Daughters and Sons in 1925. It had several cabins but the three most well-known were the Cuddle Inn, the Tumble Inn, and the Chuckle Inn. In front of the Tumble Inn cottage, from left to right, are the following: (front row) Wendy Ruggles, Sue Belcher, and Cathy Shaw; (middle row) Carol Christy, Kathy Lunt, and Lydia Fratas; (back row) Carryl Bishop (senior counselor) and Meredith Wardwell (junior counselor).

Counselors gather at Camp Wampatuck on the shore of Lake Wampatuck, or Wampatuck Pond. The senior campers who had attended Camp Wampatuck two seasons and were between the ages of 15 and 18 had the honor of staying at the E. Trask Hill Cottage across the street. These girls had special activities and privileges. Also across the street was Gordon Rest, the vacation home sponsored by the International Order of the King's Daughters and Sons. From left to right are the following: (front row) Shirley Kent, Carryl Dennis, and Sylvia Mitchell; (middle row) Carol Loman, Pat Randolph, Louise Thompson (director), Alison Robbins (assistant director), Frances Blake, and Meredith Wardwell; (back row) Cappy Parker, Janie Fratas, Aryanna Shaw, Shirley Simpson, Jane Storey, Mary O'Toole, and Carol Bishop.

Many summer cottages were on the shores of Maquan Pond. Shown here in 1902 is the Maquan Cottage, with a group of summer visitors. This cottage still exists at 72 Woodman Terrace and is called the Barrett compound.

Boating on Lake Wampatuck, or Wampatuck Pond, was a favorite pastime in Hanson. In 1695, Nathaniel Thomas bought 250 acres from the Native American Chief Wampatuck. According to legend, he received the right to use water from Maquan and Indian Head Ponds to build a dam at Indian Head Brook. For generations, this was known as Mill Pond, but it is now called Lake Wampatuck, or Wampatuck Pond, after the chief.

The fourth annual Mardi Gras celebration was held by the Teen Timers in 1956. It was held in the Memorial Auditorium inside the Indian Head School. Garland and Ruth Brooks (center foreground) chaired the affair. Teen Timers was originally organized by the Parent-Teacher Association in 1946. When the association dropped the sponsorship of the Teen Timers, Dorothy and John Davis carried it on. By 1950, membership had grown to over 200.

The Hanson Teen Timers held a Mardi Gras ball each year. In 1956, it was considered one of the important social events of the year. The Teen Timers program was open to any boy or girl from the fourth through tenth grades.

Young mothers gather together for friendship and support in 1955. From left to right are the following: (front row) Dottie Paine with Diane and Donna; Joanne Estes with Cathy; Dorothy Casoli with Janet; and Kirsti Milne with Jim and Kevin; (back row) Beth Harriott with Pam; Betty Botieri with Carol; Carmela Ibbitson with Jackie; and Virginia Fisher with Chris and Kim.

Mothers continue to gather together for friendship and support in 1960. From left to right are the following: (front row) Nan Trotta, Beth Harriott, Nancy Bergman, Betty Rich, Joanne Estes, and Peggy Bernado; (back row) Carmela Ibbitson, Kirsti Milne, Lorraine Hammond, Nola Mansfield, Claire Lincoln, Dorothy Paine, and Betty Botieri. Later, the group became known as the Hanson-Pembroke Mothers Club, which still exists today.

Residents here were "goin' to meetin' " on Sunday, May 23, 1948. The Congregational church, on High Street, officially celebrated its 200th anniversary with events from August 15 to August 31.

In 1948, the First Congregational Church of Hanson held its 200th anniversary. Shown here on May 23 are church members in period costume. From left to right are Lydia Boulanger, Ruth Rich, Norman MacDonald, Claire MacDonald, unidentified, Alice Lewis, Dan Lewis, Bertha Baresel, Myrtie Hopkins, unidentified, Ivy MacDonald, and two unidentified women.

The policeman's ball was held at Camp Kiwanis on June 5, 1954. The camp was still owned by the Camp Fire Girls, as shown in the sign at the top of the picture. From left to right are Norma Holt, Bob McNamara, Hazel and Bob Brown, unidentified, Alfred Pillsbury, and Esther and Kenneth MacKenzie.

Out for a night on the town in 1958 are the police chiefs from area towns and their wives. From left to right are the following: (front row) Josephine Lanzillotta, Mary Levings, Howard Levings (Hanover chief of police), Norma Johnson, Ad Johnson (Rockland chief of police), Esther MacKenzie, and Olive Reid; (back row) Al Lanzillotta (Pembroke chief of police), Ken MacKenzie (Hanson chief of police), and Alvin Reid.

Hanson's 150th anniversary celebration parade was held on July 19, 1970. Shown in front of the Ocean Spray Cranberry Company building is the Masonic Wampatuck Lodge A.F. & A.M. Float. It contained cranberry picking and processing tools made in Hanson.

The Ocean Spray Cranberry Company headquarters is shown decorated with patriotic flags for Hanson's 150th anniversary. The parade route started from this Main Street building.

This float in Hanson's 150th anniversary parade was from the Indian Trail Cranberry Bogs. Located in Hanson, these bogs are owned by the Stillman family on Elm Street.

It appears that most of Hanson has gathered on the town hall lawn on July 19, 1970, waiting for the parade to go by. The town hall was decorated with flags for the anniversary celebration.

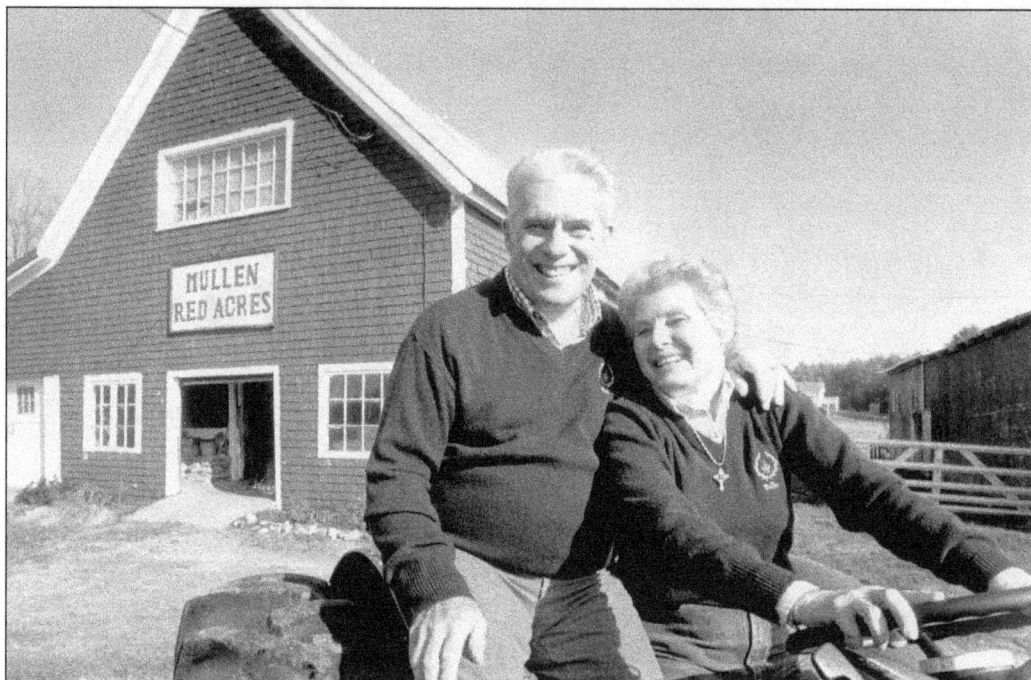

George and Mary Mullen began hosting the Christmas Sing on Red Acres Farm in 1955, and it has been a tradition ever since. The Christmas Sing has grown each year and now includes all of the Mullen extended family as hosts, including the Gerry Lozeau family, the John Norris family, the Bob Scandurra family, and the Michael Mullen family. Also lending a hand each year are the 4-H Club and the Hanson Kiwanis Club.

The annual Christmas Sing offers a crèche scene, a bonfire, hot popcorn, marshmallow toasting, hot coffee, hot chocolate, Christmas carols, and lots of fun and good cheer. The event adds memories that people cherish the most. It has been held at Red Acres Farm, located at 517 West Washington Street, for more than 45 years.

Shown is the Hanson A.A. Little League team of 1966. From left to right are the following: (first row) unidentified, Rick Raymond, Ron Butterfield, Nick Gardner, and Chuck Rasch; (second row) John Crowley, unidentified, Neal Downey, and Jack Ferry; (third row) Tim Crowley, Joe Shields, Rocky Westberg, and Mike Danner; (fourth row) coaches Thomas Butterfield, James Kehoe, and Donald Botieri.

Shown is the 1969 midgets team of the Hanson Pee Wee League. From left to right are the following: (front row) Richard Lawson, Tom Kirwan, Jeff Hammond, Ted Keary, Brian Snow, Ronnie Butterfield, Scott Siereveld, Mike Wallace, Steve Smart, and Paul Milk; (back row) Wally Darsch (coach), Doug Paulding, Eddie Coulstring, Matt Glynn, Tom Hancock, Joe Shields, Jack Ferry, Freddie Pike, Dave Brinkert, George Ibbitson, and coaches Dave Snow and Bud Smith.

Hanson girls appeared in the annual Parent-Teacher Association minstrel show in 1950. From left to right are Patricia Libby, Eleanor Bates, Sara Dunbar, Dorothy Coffey, Lorraine Tassinari, and Joanne Brooks.

Adolph Scott was a farmer, father, grandfather, logger, truck driver, shipyard worker, milkman, carpenter by trade, and hay and sleigh ride entrepreneur. He ran hay rides and sleigh rides from his home at 360 Indian Head Street. He built his own wagon, and Pinty and Pete, his dapple grey Percheron horses, were very well known in this area. Oftentimes, his wagon, draped in bunting, would show up at the Fourth of July parade.

Visit us at
arcadiapublishing.com

....

www.ingramcontent.com/pod-product-compliance
Lightning Source LLC
Chambersburg PA
CBHW050630110426
42813CB00007B/1766